101 Dynamite Answers to Interview Questions

Books and CD-ROMs by Drs. Ron and Caryl Krannich

101 Dynamite Answers to Interview Questions
201 Dynamite Job Search Letters
The Almanac of International Jobs and Careers
Best Jobs For the 1990s and Into the 21st Century
Change Your Job, Change Your Life
The Complete Guide to International Jobs and Careers
The Complete Guide to Public Employment
The Directory of Federal Jobs and Employers
Discover the Best Jobs For You!
Dynamite Cover Letters
Dynamite Networking For Dynamite Jobs
Dynamite Résumés
Dynamite Salary Negotiations
Dynamite Tele-Search
The Educator's Guide to Alternative Jobs and Careers
Find a Federal Job Fast!
From Air Force Blue to Corporate Gray
From Army Green to Corporate Gray
From Navy Blue to Corporate Gray
High Impact Résumés and Letters
Interview For Success
Job-Power Source CD-ROM
Jobs and Careers With Nonprofit Organizations
Jobs For People Who Love Travel
Mayors and Managers
Moving Out of Education
Moving Out of Government
The Politics of Family Planning Policy
Re-Careering in Turbulent Times
Résumés and Cover Letters For Transitioning Military Personnel
Shopping and Traveling in Exotic Asia
Shopping in Exciting Australia and Papua New Guinea
Shopping in Exotic Places
Shopping the Exotic South Pacific
Treasures and Pleasures of Australia
Treasures and Pleasures of China
Treasures and Pleasures of Hong Kong
Treasures and Pleasures of Indonesia
Treasures and Pleasures of Italy
Treasures and Pleasures of Paris and the French Riviera
Treasures and Pleasures of Singapore and Malaysia
Treasures and Pleasures of Thailand
Ultimate Job Source CD-ROM

101 Dynamite Answers To Interview Questions

Sell Your Strengths!

Caryl Rae Krannich, Ph.D.
Ronald L. Krannich, Ph.D.

Third Edition

IMPACT PUBLICATIONS
Manassas Park, VA

101 DYNAMITE ANSWERS TO INTERVIEW QUESTIONS: Sell Your Strengths!

Library of Congress Cataloging-in-Publication Data

Krannich, Caryl Rae
   101 dynamite answers to interview questions: sell your strengths!
Caryl Rae Krannich, Ronald L. Krannich.
     p. cm.
   Rev. ed. of: Dynamite answers to interview questions. 2nd ed.
c1994.
   Includes bibliographical references and index.
   ISBN 1-57023-078-1
   1. Employment interviewing. 2. Krannich, Ronald L.
II. Krannich, Caryl Rae. Dynamite answers to interview questions.
III. Title.
HF5549.5.I6K69   1997
650.14—dc21   97-16952
                                         CIP

Contents

Dedicated in loving memory to

Caryl's brother

David Wayne Woodring
(Colonel USAF)

1947-1992

A dynamite attorney

A dynamite officer

And a dynamite brother, son, husband and father.

He is greatly loved,

greatly admired

and greatly missed.

101 Dynamite Answers to Interview Questions

1

No More Sweaty Palms!

What are the first thoughts that come to mind as you contemplate a job interview? Is the surge of joy you feel at having a chance at the job—a chance to demonstrate to the interviewer that you are the person who should be hired—overshadowed by feelings of nervousness? Do your fears of sweaty palms, a dry mouth, churning stomach, and wobbly knees leave you less than enthusiastic? If your answers to these questions are "yes," you have lots of company, and lots to learn.

However, since a successful job interview is a prerequisite for most jobs, it makes sense to find ways to turn interview apprehension into interview anticipation. That's what this book is all about.

Interviews Count the Most

Interviews don't just count—they count the most. Take yourself back a few weeks. Maybe you wrote a terrific resume and cover letter, networked with the right people, invited yourself to the

1

interview through sheer persistence, or just had a stroke of good luck. Whatever methods you used, congratulations; you are a "winner" at this stage of the job search. You've become successful at what others only dream of achieving—grabbing the interest and attention of employers who decide it's now time to see you in person. They need to further evaluate your qualifications to determine if you will fit into their organization.

> # The job interview is the prerequisite to getting the job.

But it's now a whole new ball game. While writing resumes, following job leads, and contacting employers are very important job search activities, the job interview is what really counts. Indeed, the job interview is **the** prerequisite to getting the job. No job interview, no job offer. No job offer, no job. You simply must perform well in the job interview if you are to land the job.

The skills you used in writing, distributing, and following-up your resumes and letters, researching companies, and networking helped get you an invitation to meet hiring officials in person. You now have a personal invitation—the door is open for you to meet those who have the power to hire. Now you must demonstrate another set of important skills once inside that door—your ability to conduct an effective interview. This means knowing how to best handle the interview situation and the interview process. It involves everything from greeting the hiring official and managing questions to following-up the interview within 48 hours.

Exchanging Information

The main purpose of the job interview is to exchange information about you, the job, and the employer. You do this by answering and asking questions both verbally and nonverbally. This is a serious business—the employer's money in exchange for your talent. Therefore, you need to learn as much as possible about each other before making any long-term commitments. This is not the time for playing any get-the-job games.

The process of answering and asking questions for you involves two important and sometimes contradictory considerations:

1. **Get the job:** You must sufficiently impress hiring officials both professionally and personally so you will be offered the job.

2. **Get useful information:** You must acquire critical information on whether or not you wish to join the organization. In other words, the employer must also sufficiently impress you before you will accept a job offer.

These two considerations often compete with one other because of interview apprehension. Apprehension about the interview situation—complete with a dry throat, sweaty palms, and wobbly knees—leads some interviewees to concentrate solely on playing the "good interviewee" role to the exclusion of acquiring important information for decision-making. Fearing they will not sufficiently impress the interviewer, they become preoccupied with dressing right and giving "model" answers to interview questions rather than concentrating on exchanging information and learning about the job and the employer. They communicate anything but their real selves to employers.

You should not let this happen to you. After all, you owe it to yourself, and perhaps others close to you, to make sound career decisions. The job interview is not a time for you to be someone else. Like your resume, your interview behavior should represent the "unique you" to employers. This is the time to present your best self in the process of learning about the job and the employer.

Throughout this book we stress the importance of lowering your apprehension, raising your anticipation, and focusing on the main purpose of the interview—exchanging information that will help you make a critical **career decision** as well as assist the employer in making an important **hiring decision**.

Prepare Your "Best Self"

The skills involved in answering and asking interview questions are not something you acquire overnight by reading a book on how to conduct effective job interviews. They are **communication skills you already possess** but which you may not have used for a while. What you need to do is refocus and sharpen those skills in relation to a clear understanding of how the interview process unfolds and what you are expected to do in the interview situation.

Indeed, you want to prepare well for all types of questions you are likely to be asked as well as identify several questions you need to ask of the employer. This preparation involves everything from anticipating certain types of questions and maintaining a positive attitude to expressing a particular answering style and presenting positive content in your answers. For you want to be honest in everything you say and do. This by no means implies you should be either naive nor stupid in what you say by confessing your weaknesses to hiring officials. You need to stress what is right about you—your strengths and achievements—those patterns that determine and support your success. This is what you should concentrate on when preparing for the interview—presenting your very best self to employers who are interested in hiring your major strengths.

Without this preparation, you may not be able to present your "best self" to the employer. Your dry throat, sweaty palms, and wobbly knees may take center stage as you make numerous interview mistakes that prevent you from both impressing the employer and acquiring useful information. That would be unfortunate since you have already come a long way toward landing the job. Whatever you do, don't short-change yourself by not preparing well for possible interview questions.

You Need to Both Answer and Ask

This is what this book is all about—learning to sharpen communication skills you already possess in relation to the interview situation and the interview process. You'll learn to present your best self to employers. We'll show you how to make a smooth transition from your resume to the job offer. You'll answer and ask questions that both impress employers and generate important information to assist you in determining if indeed this job is the right "fit" for you.

Let's be perfectly clear what this book is not about. It is **not** a book on how you can take charge of the interview situation. That would be presumptuous and you would probably become either overbearing or obnoxious, or both. It is **not** a book on how to pull the wool over the eyes of the employer by arriving "dressed for success" and then dishing out "canned answers" to interview questions. That would be dishonest. And this is **not** a book about how to cleverly manipulate the interviewer to your advantage. That would be unethical, it assumes the interviewer is stupid, and the technique probably would not work.

This is a book about some of the most important communication of your life. Doing well in a 30 to 60 minute interview can have several positive outcomes for you and your career.

Create Your Own Interview Power

You can acquire the power to turn interview apprehension into interview anticipation and success. In the following chapters we will share with you the secrets to interview success. We will focus on you in relationship to the employer—what you both need to do in order to arrive at a mutually satisfactory arrangement that will hopefully lead to a satisfying long-term professional and personal relationship.

Our approach to this subject is very simple. We begin with you, the interviewee, and move you directly into and through the interview process, from beginning to end. For the most part, the chapters flow in the same manner as the job interview—a sequence of different interview questions you need to both answer and ask.

We begin in **Chapter 2**, "Interview Types and Techniques," by analyzing the interview situation—types of interviews you can expect to encounter as well as the structure of job interviews. We believe much of your apprehension is related to these structural questions. The more you know about the types of situations you are likely to encounter, the better prepared you should be for answering and asking questions both verbally and nonverbally.

In **Chapter 3**, "45 Key Interview Principles," we turn our attention to a comprehensive set of interview principles that form the basis for effective interviewing. These principles are much more than just a scattering of hot tips, generic experiences, common sense knowledge, or structured logic. Based on research and experience, they are a well integrated set of principles that define effective communication in most professional and social settings. Our principles cover three distinct interview stages you will most likely encounter during your job search:

- interview preparation

- interview encounters

- interview follow-ups

Taken together, these principles also constitute a well-defined **strategy** for conducting a dynamite job interview. They are your tickets to interview success.

In **Chapter 4**, "Preparing For the Interview," we examine important interview preparation steps that go beyond just practicing model answers and questions. You'll examine strategies and learn to anticipate interview scenarios in this critical chapter that serves as a transition to the actual job interview.

We then turn our attention to the nuts-and-bolts of job interviews—specific questions and answers. Based on our principles of effective interviewing, in **Chapter 5**—"Dynamite Answers: The Verbal Component"—we examine the verbal components of the interview—the art of speaking well and the most common questions asked of interviewees. Each question is followed with examples of **dynamite answer strategies** that will both impress interviewers and generate useful information for decision-making purposes. These clearly illustrate our interviewing principles.

In **Chapter 6**—"Dynamite Visuals: The Nonverbal Component"—we turn to an equally important but often neglected element in effective interviewing—the critical nonverbal components of the interview. Again, based on our principles in Chapter 3, we discuss dynamite visuals which constitute another important channel for answering interview questions. These nonverbal components are constantly affecting answers to interview questions. Indeed, they often answer many nonverbalized questions the interviewer prefers not asking, because they may be illegal, or they appear unprofessional or embarrassing to both ask and answer. You need to know about this silent language so your nonverbal messages are the most appropriate possible. We'll show you how to communicate at this level without uttering a single word. You may be surprised to discover your nonverbal answers to interview questions are sometimes more important than your verbal answers! This being the case, Chapter 6 addresses many important interview behaviors.

Chapter 7—"Dynamite Questions You Should Ask"—turns the interview table. The focus of attention shifts from questions about you to questions concerning the job and the employer. While you will primarily answer questions during the job interview, you also must be prepared to ask questions. After all, you need information about the job and employer. You will gain some of this information when responding to the interviewer's questions, but you should prepare a set of questions that address your most important concerns. Interviewers expect you to ask intelligent questions which demonstrate your interest in the job and enthusiasm for the employer. In fact, the more you find out about the job and the concerns of management, the better you can focus your responses to their needs. This chapter identifies numerous questions you should ask in the process of both favorably impressing the interviewer and gathering useful information.

Chapter 8—"Dynamite Follow-Ups"—completes our examination of dynamite answers to interview questions. This final chapter is the critical action chapter. Here we address a much neglected aspect of the job search—effective interview follow-up methods. It's based upon a simple truism: you won't get the job offer until the employer takes action beyond the question and answer interview encounter. There are certain things you can do to help the person reach a decision, from follow-up telephone calls to thank-you letters. We identify the best follow-up methods as well as provide some telephone dialogues and model thank-you letters for your reference.

Chapter 9—"101 Answers You Should Formulate"—presents a comprehensive checklist by category of the 101 sample interview questions and answers addressed throughout the book as well as provides a useful orientation on how to best handle each of the questions. The chapter is organized in this manner so you can review some of the most important job interview questions and suggested answers based upon the 45 principles we outlined in Chapter 3. If you need to prepare for a job interview that's coming up in a few days, this chapter will assist you in getting quickly organized.

Taken together, these chapters constitute a crash course in effective job interview skills. Ideally you should complete this book early in your job search. However, chances are you are reading it in preparation for an impending job interview, which may be in another day or two! If this is your situation, we strongly recommend focusing on the principles of effective interviewing as outlined in Chapter 3. These principles emphasize a particular attitude and orientation you need to consistently present through-out the interview as well as during the follow-up phase. These principles will help you formulate answers to the many standard interview questions you will need to address without sounding like you have prepared "canned" answers. They also will help you handle the secret language of interview success.

Avoid Easy Temptations

One important word of caution is in order before you proceed further into this book. Whatever you do, don't try to memorize canned answers to interview questions. Succumbing to such a temptation will probably produce negative outcomes for you. This approach is likely to turn off interviewers who know you are being less than forthcoming; it may even raise questions about your honesty and integrity. In addition, your nonverbal communication may negate the messages you intend to communicate at the "canned" verbal level. Our examples of effective answers are presented to **illustrate the principles** in Chapter 3 that should guide you through each step of the job interview process—preparation, presentation, and follow-up.

Choose the Right Resources

This book is primarily concerned with communicating critical job and career information to employers in face-to-face job interview situations. Each year millions of job hunters turn to career planning books for assistance. Many begin with a general book and next turn to resume and interview books. Others begin with a resume book and later seek other types of job resources, including letter writing and networking books. Some go directly to computer software programs and CD-ROMs or visit various World Wide Web sites on the Internet for producing resumes and preparing for job interviews.

If this book represents your first career planning book, you may want to supplement it with a few other key books. Many of these books are available in your local library and bookstore or they can be ordered directly from Impact Publications (see the "Career Resources" sections at the end of this book). Most of these resources, along with hundreds of others, are available through Impact's comprehensive "Career Warehouse and Superstore" on the World Wide Web:

http://www.impactpublications.com

Impact's site also includes new titles, specials, and job search tips for keeping you in touch with the latest in career information and resources. You also can request a free copy of their career catalog by sending a self-addressed stamped envelope (#10 business size) to have it mailed to you. Send your request to:

IMPACT PUBLICATIONS
ATTN: Free Career Catalog
9104-N Manassas Drive
Manassas Park, VA 20111-2366

Put Dynamite Into Your Interviews

Whatever you do, make sure you acquire, use, and taste the fruits of dynamite answers to interview questions. You should go into the job interview equipped with the necessary knowledge and skills to be most effective in communicating your qualifications to employers and acquiring important information on both the job and the employer.

As you will quickly discover, the job market is not a place to engage in wishful thinking. It's at times impersonal, frequently ego deflating, and often unforgiving of errors. It requires clear thinking, strong organizational skills, and effective strategies for making the right moves with employers. Above all, it rewards individuals who follow-through in implementing each job search step with enthusiasm, dogged persistence, and the ability to handle rejections.

May you soon discover this power and incorporate it in your own dynamite answers to interview questions!

2

Interview Types and Techniques

Job seekers and advice givers alike often talk about "the job interview" as if it were a single entity—always the same and with a single set of expectations on the part of both the interviewer and interviewee. In reality, the interpersonal dynamics change as the participants and the situation change, and each interview is different from any other.

Variable Situations

Interviews involve numerous variables—the interviewer's and interviewee's goals, personality, and approach; types of interview; interview settings; questioning techniques; and interview structure. Since each of these variables will affect both your answers/ questions and interview outcome, you must be aware of changing interview situations and handle each variable in the best manner possible.

While many interviewees expect interviewers are in the driver's seat—intelligent, confident, competent, and in control—in fact many interviewers have no training in interviewing—let alone personnel interviewing. They may be unsure or hesitant of themselves, asking many questions that may be irrelevant to the job under consideration or simply restating information contained in the applicant's resume. If the interviewer is from outside the personnel department, he may conduct interviews infrequently. If he is from the operational unit, rather than personnel, he may view the time consumed to conduct an interview as taking valuable time away from the work at hand. He may also feel very uncomfortable doing something—conducting the interview—that he knows he doesn't do well. In other words, he is far from being in the driver's seat. Indeed, you may have to help him through the interview!

Although there are several different interview types and each interview is different from any other, there are enough similarities for each type of interview that one should be able to develop a set of expectations that will be useful.

Let's describe the interview situation in comprehensive terms. We include several types of interviews along with interviewers' and interviewees' goals and various interview settings, questioning techniques, and structures you are most likely to encounter. These variables are outlined and related to one another in the diagram on page 14.

This chapter should help you identify the types of playing fields you will most likely encounter with a single employer or with many different employers. You will quickly discover interview skills involve a great deal more than learning appropriate answers to expected interview questions. At the very least you must be prepared to encounter many different types and settings for interviews, which may involve anything from climbing out of the shower to answer a telephone call that unexpectedly becomes a screening interview to encountering a panel of interviewers who

INTERVIEW SITUATION: TYPES, SETTINGS, QUESTIONING TECHNIQUES AND STRUCTURE

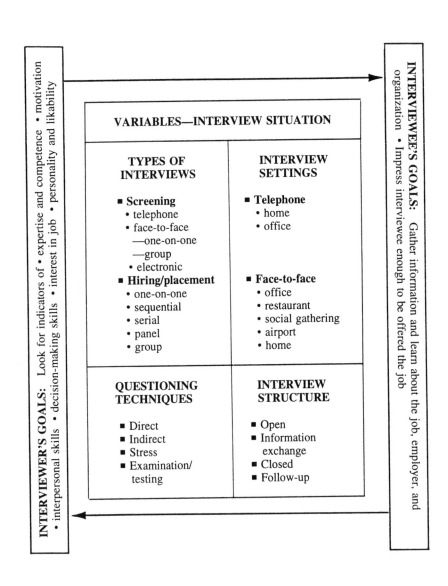

INTERVIEWER'S GOALS: Look for indicators of • expertise and competence • motivation • interpersonal skills • decision-making skills • interest in job • personality and likability

INTERVIEWEE'S GOALS: Gather information and learn about the job, employer, and organization • Impress interviewee enough to be offered the job

VARIABLES—INTERVIEW SITUATION

TYPES OF INTERVIEWS

- **Screening**
  - telephone
  - face-to-face
    —one-on-one
    —group
  - electronic
- **Hiring/placement**
  - one-on-one
  - sequential
  - serial
  - panel
  - group

INTERVIEW SETTINGS

- **Telephone**
  - home
  - office
- **Face-to-face**
  - office
  - restaurant
  - social gathering
  - airport
  - home

QUESTIONING TECHNIQUES

- Direct
- Indirect
- Stress
- Examination/ testing

INTERVIEW STRUCTURE

- Open
- Information exchange
- Closed
- Follow-up

engage you in a two-hour stress interview. You also must be prepared for different questioning techniques as well as the overall structure and flow of the interview. These variables will both grow out of and affect the goals of both you and the interviewer. They will have an important impact on the outcome of the interview that goes far beyond the content of interview questions and answers.

This chapter should help you identify the types of playing fields you will most likely encounter with a single employer or with many different employers. You will quickly discover interview skills involve a great deal more than learning appropriate answers to expected interview questions. At the very least you must be prepared to encounter many differ-ent types and settings for inter-views, which may involve anything from climbing out of the shower to answer a telephone call that unex-pectedly becomes a screening inter-view to encountering a panel of interviewers who engage you in a two-hour stress interview. You also must be prepared for different questioning techniques as well as

> **Interview skills involve a great deal more than learning appropriate answers to expected interview questions.**

the overall structure and flow of the interview. These are variables which will both grow out of and affect the goals of both you and the interviewer. They will have an important impact on the outcome of the interview that goes far beyond the content of interview questions and answers.

Interviewer Goals and Expectations

The interviewer expects that an applicant who is invited to an interview will be at his best—both in appearance and behavior.

You will have conducted basic research on the company and will be able to both answer and ask questions that relate to your skills and goals as they relate to the job under consideration.

The interviewer has certain goals she must achieve through the interview process. She will control many of the variables affecting the interview situation in order to achieve those goals. First, the interviewer looks for indicators of the applicant's **expertise and competence**—your skills, knowledge and abilities as they relate to the job. Since your education and past work experience are factors that would have been apparent on your resume, the basic requirements for consideration for the position have been met or you wouldn't have been invited to the interview. But now the employer wants specifics that go beyond the degrees earned, jobs held, and duties performed. Specifics that indicate what you can do for the employer in **her** organization.

Second, the interviewer is interested in indicators of the applicant's **motivation**. Expertise is an important consideration, but your drive and energy may be what set you apart from others and gives you an edge in the hiring process. The employer wants to know about your potential for development. Are you motivated to learn new skills and ways of doing things?

Third, your **interpersonal skills** also are of concern. Someone who can do the job, but doesn't fit into the work setting, isn't a valuable employee. Your ability to get along with co-workers is not always easy to discern, but something the interviewer will be trying to assess. How well do you take supervision? Are you able to follow orders from those in positions to direct you? And if you are hired in a track that may lead to your becoming a supervisor, your leadership skills will also be important.

Fourth, the applicant's **decision-making and problem-solving abilities** will be important for many positions. How well are you able to deal with an out-of-the-ordinary situation you may encounter on the job? Will you be able to distinguish between those situations where innovation is required and those where established procedures must be followed? Can you quickly deal with a situation by analyzing the nature of the issue and taking appropriate action that incorporates alternative courses of action?

Fifth, at the same time that the interviewer is attempting to discern your skills to do the work as well as fit into the corporate structure, she is also trying to assess your real **interest** in the job and the firm. Will you be a dedicated and loyal employee? Or do you merely see this job as a way-station on your way to something bigger and better somewhere else?

Sixth, while you may think employers are mainly concerned with assessing your job performance skills, they also are interested in your **personality or likability**. They prefer working with people they like. After all, likable people are those that tend to get along well with others. How well do you relate to the interviewer? Do you listen well, give positive verbal and nonverbal feedback, have a pleasant and enthusiastic manner, and demonstrate a sense of humor and smile? Or do you tend to be negative, boring, and unenthusiastic? Employers look for energetic personalities who also tend to transfer their energy into their work.

Interviewee Goals and Expectations

Interviewee's also have specific goals relevant to the interview situation. Your major goals are to gain information about the job, employer, and organization and demonstrate how your skills, knowledge and abilities will fit the needs of the organization. You want to impress the interviewer enough to be offered the job. You expect the interviewer to take the lead in determining the structure of the interview, but you also need to structure your behavior in such a manner that it affects both the interview situation and the final outcome.

Most interviewees have little knowledge of the various types of interviews or the variety of settings and forms that an interview may take. The information in this chapter is designed to provide a basis for understanding the various interviews you may face. Granted, no two interviews are the same, but it is possible to classify interviews in ways that should enhance your understanding of what is happening if you encounter a situation that doesn't quite fit into your perceptual expectations as to what constitutes a job interview.

Interview Types/Goals

There are two basic types of interviews with which the job-seeker needs some familiarity: the **informational interview** and the **employment interview**. The informational interview results from the networking process. You should talk with people in your area of interest and identify persons who are in a position to share information with you about your potential field of employment. Once you have identified persons who are likely to have useful information, you want to contact them and try to arrange informational interviews. As the name implies, you are not seeking a job from these people—only information and advice that will be useful to you later in your job search.

Informational Interviews

Your goal in an informational interview will be to pose questions about such things as opportunities in "X" field—at the entry-level or at whatever level you expect to enter the field; the likelihood of advancement; what changes are taking place within the field that will affect things such as hiring needs, special skills, degrees or certification necessary for employment; special problems facing workers in "X" field; salary levels in your geographical area in "X" field—both at your anticipated entry level and as you advance. You will probably want to ask questions about various companies in your area that are hiring workers in your field. Your goal is to find out as much as you can about your field and the organizations that are hiring—or are likely to hire in the future—people in your field of employment.

For more information on informational interviews, you may wish to consult another of our interview books, *Interview For Success*. Since the informational interview is a particular type of interview in which you become the interviewer, we only mention this type of interview in passing here. However, it's an extremely important type of interview in one's overall job search; indeed, it may be the single most important job search activity for making contacts with potential employers who may later invite you to a job interview. However, our main focus in this book is the employment interview where you primarily play the role of interviewee in the process of getting a job offer.

Employment Interviews

Employment interviews may take several forms. If your job search takes you to many interviews, you are likely to encounter more than one interview format. Employment formats may be best divided into two major categories—screening interviews and hiring/placement interviews.

Screening Interviews

Screening interviews may take place over the telephone or in a face-to-face setting. **Face-to-face** screening interviews are usually held somewhere other than the employer's offices. In a college setting, interviews may be held in conjunction with the office of career planning and placement. Screening interviews may be a part of the activities involved with a job fair held in a hotel or other neutral place and in which many potential employers take part. Not limited to private industry, the federal government has also been holding many job fairs over recent years.

Most face-to-face screening interviews are also one-on-one— one applicant talking with one hiring official. However, some organizations that are deluged with applications for certain positions, such as the airlines for flight attendants, may bring 20-30 people together at one time. In this situation the employer is able to screen far more people in less time than if they scheduled them each for individual interviews.

Those applicants who are screened "in" as a result of the group screening interview are invited back for an individual hiring interview.

Screening interviews, as the name implies, provide employers the opportunity to make initial decisions as to whether they want to further interview an applicant. It helps them narrow the field of applicants to a more manageable number for conducting formal face-to-face job interviews. In other words, applicants are screened "in" or "out" of further consideration. Job offers are seldom an immediate result of a screening interview.

Telephone screening interviews are one of the least understood interview formats. Because many applicants are unprepared or do not understand their purpose, they do poorly. Many employers use telephone interviews these days. Such interviews are more time efficient and cost effective in eliminating a large number of applicants than face-to-face interviews. While the telephone interview may take only five to ten minutes, an office interview may take an hour or more. The telephone interview is especially cost effective when applicants are from out of town since it saves the expense of bringing several in for face-to-face interviews.

Since employers can be expected to conduct screening interviews with greater and greater frequency as interview costs increase, it pays to be prepared when the telephone rings.

If you receive an initial phone call from an employer, assume you are being screened for a later face-to-face interview. Take this telephone interview as seriously as you would one in any other format. What you say and how you say it will probably determine whether you will be invited to a hiring/placement interview.

With this in mind, it is advisable to have an area by your telephone equipped with everything you will need to come through the unexpected screening interview with flying colors. A pad of paper, pen, copy of your resume, a calendar (with commitments noted) are basic elements. It is also a good idea to have a list of the organizations which you have contacted in your job search; the names of individuals to whom you have sent your resume (or talked to previously) listed; and a folder or notebook with copies of all your job search correspondence organized alphabetically by company.

Keep the essential elements you need to be prepared for the telephone interview available at any location where you are likely to receive a call from a potential employer. If you have listed both your home and work numbers on your resume or application, you could receive a call at either place. If your present employer doesn't know you are engaged in a job search, you may wish to keep your interview essentials organized in your briefcase in the event you get a call at work. However, if you have no private place at your office where you could conceivably talk on the phone, you may prefer to ask potential employers not to call you at your present place of employment. Alternatively, you may want to ask the interviewer if you could call her back at a specific time— convenient to the interviewer—since you are in the middle of an important meeting. This will give you time to collect your thoughts and find a more private location from which to conduct the telephone screening interview.

At this point the interviewer is looking for reasons to knock people out of further consideration. For example, she may ask you to clarify some points in your resume concerning experience as well as inquire about your availability and salary expectations:

When you say you have *"six years of progressive experience handling all aspects of quality control with XYZ Company,"* what does that mean in terms of the number of employees you supervised? How did your responsibilities increase?

Would you be ready to start work in another three weeks?

What are your salary expectations?

Be very careful how you answer these screening questions, especially the one on salary expectations. Factual questions, such as the first one, deserve factual answers along with some positive contextual comments. For example, try to put your supervisory skills into some **performance context**, such as

I supervised six people. We were able to improve product quality by 50 percent which resulted in 25 percent fewer customer complaints.

On the question of availability, use you own judgment. Remember, you should give your present employer at least two weeks notice. If the job requires a major geographic move, you may need more time. For now you may want to answer "Yes" knowing full well you need to work out the details with both your current and future employer. If you say "No," you inject a negative into this interview that may eliminate you from further consideration.

As for salary expectations, the rule is to keep this question to the very end of the job interview—after you learn the **worth** of the position and demonstrate your **value** to employers. Answer by saying you are "open" at this point. You need to know more about the position. If the interviewer persists, turn the question around and ask "What is the current range for this position for someone with my qualifications?" And if the person continues to persist for a figure, give them a salary range you know will fit into their budget as well as your expectations: "I was thinking in the range of $43,000 to $50,000." Base your responses to salary questions on information gained from your research. This is not the time to resort to wishful thinking.

The person conducting the screening interview has a negative goal as far as the applicant is concerned. The interviewer wants to eliminate as many candidates as possible from further consideration so the hiring/placement interview can be conducted with a more manageable number of applicants. On the other hand, your goal is to be to included in the final pool of candidates. What you say in this screening interview will be very important in moving you into the select group of applicants.

The telephone screening interview is primarily a verbal encounter, but it also includes numerous nonverbal components. Make sure you speak up, use good grammar, speak in complete sentences, avoid vocalized pauses and fillers, are decisive and positive, and inject enthusiasm and energy into your telephone voice. If your voice tends to be high-pitched over the telephone, try to lower it somewhat. You want to sound interesting enough so the interviewer will want to see you in person. If your grammar is poor, if you sound indecisive, lack enthusiasm, or have a high-pitched and squeaky voice, the interviewer may screen you out of further consideration regardless of what you say in response to his questions or how terrific your resume looks. He will have "a gut feeling" that he doesn't want to interview you because you just don't sound right for the job.

New Electronic Screening Interview

A relatively new method for screening job applicants is the use of computerized questions to elicit information before the applicant meets with the hiring official. The applicant is initially asked to sit at a computer terminal and respond to a series of questions that will also be "scored" electronically. Though in limited use at present, and used primarily by larger firms, the method may "catch on." If you face this situation, you should do better if you have some understanding of what is happening to you.

Employers who use this method believe electronic screening has several advantages. First, the computer presentation poses exactly the same questions in the same way to all applicants and will "score" the responses thus supposedly taking some of the subjectivity out of this portion of the interview. Second, the computer can "score" your responses quickly. If several questions are designed with purposeful redundancy in order to identify the individual who is not responding honestly but trying to skew the results a certain way, the computerized scoring will identify the inconsistencies and this information will be available to the human interviewer who conducts the subsequent face-to-face interview. In some instances the scoring programs are designed so that inconsistencies in responses as well as response rates are noted. In other words, if you take a significantly longer time to answer certain questions than is **your** norm for the majority of questions, the questions you pondered excessively will be noted.

The interviewer whom you meet with following your session at the computer terminal will no doubt probe areas in which your responses or response rate seemed to indicate inconsistencies or longer than usual hesitations. The interviewer will assume that you may have problems or something to hide in these areas. If you have read the following sections in this book which help you prepare for interview questions and how to present your responses in an honest, yet positive manner, you should be able to handle the face-to-face follow-up to the electronic screening interview.

Although many employers may initially jump on the band-wagon and move into what they consider to be the progressive new interview methodology—electronic screening interviews—we suspect it may be fraught with problems that will slow its general use. Aside from the expense which may not be justified for many smaller firms, it seems to be a modern method of presenting traditional personality testing.

Two decades ago many firms used paper-and-pencil tests to access applicants' personality traits. After several court cases in which employers could not demonstrate a bonafide relationship between the tests and the jobs for which applicants were being screened, employers quietly dropped the use of most of these tests. A similar fate may be in store for these new electronic tests.

Hiring/Placement Interviews

Once you make it through the screening interview—if there has been one—you go on to the **real** interviews. There are five basic formats for hiring interviews. Most any interview will fall into one of these categories or be a combination of more than one of them. They are one-to-one, sequential, serial, panel, or group interviews.

One-to-One Interviews

One-to-one, face-to-face interviews are the most common type faced by interviewees. The applicant and the employer meet, usually at the employer's office, and sit down to discuss the position and the applicant's skills, knowledge, and abilities as they relate to the job. At some point, though hopefully late in the interview, salary considerations as well as other benefits will be discussed.

While a screening interview is often conducted by someone in personnel—after all, screening is one of their major functions—hiring decisions are usually made by department managers for lower and many mid-level positions, and by upper management for top-level positions. If the hiring interview is conducted by someone from the department which has the position, you can expect the interviewer to ask many specific job-content questions. If the interviewer is from personnel, the questions will tend to be more general.

Sequential Interviews

For many positions, especially those beyond entry-level, more than one interview will be necessary. Sequential interviews are simply a series of interviews with the decision being made to screen the candidate in or out after each interview. The candidates who are screened in are called back for additional interviews. Although each of the sequential interviews is most frequently a one-to-one interview, you could meet with more than one interviewer at the same time in any of these sessions. You may meet with the same person in each interview, but it is more likely you will meet with new people in subsequent interviews.

When sequential interviews are held, many of the terms of employment issues such as salary and benefits may not be discussed in the initial interview. These considerations may be saved until later interviews—after the pool of candidates has been narrowed and the employer is getting serious about only a very few candidates. This can work to your advantage since with each interview you should have the opportunity to find out more about the position—ask in subsequent interviews some things you wish you had asked, but forgot, in your initial interview. You also have a greater chance to demonstrate your qualifications and try to convince the interviewer(s) that you are the person for the job.

Serial Interviews

Serial interviews also consist of several interviews, one after the other. However, with serial interviews the series has been set up from the time the interview was scheduled and no decision will be made until all the interviews have been completed. Usually each meeting is with a different person or group of people, and all the interviews will be held over a one or two day period. Following these interviews, the individuals you met with will get together to compare notes and make a collective hiring decision.

Panel Interviews

Panel interviews occur infrequently, but it is possible you could encounter a situation that included this format. As the name implies, in a panel interview you are interviewed by several people at the same time. Panel interviews, are by their very nature, more stressful than most other types. At its best, you are facing several people at the same time, trying to respond to the questions of one panel member as you try to balance your perceptions of the other members' expectations. At its worst, it can be a pressure-cooker atmosphere as you are subjected to a barrage of questions, some of which may seem hostile.

Group Interviews

Though perhaps the least common of our interview types, group interviews do take place. If you find yourself being interviewed along with several other applicants, you are in a group interview.

Employers use the group setting to gain information not thought to be readily ascertained in a one-to-one interview.

In group interviews the employer will observe the interpersonal skills of the applicants. How well a candidate interacts with peers —the other applicants—is thought to be an indicator of how well the individual will get along with co-workers.

Often a question will be posed to the group or the group will be presented a problem to solve. If an applicant exhibits positive leadership and/or followership behaviors in the group setting, employers tend to believe that person will respond in similar ways in the workplace. The employer will be looking for positive skills—the ability of an interviewee to draw other candidates into the discussion, to listen to others' points of view, to ask questions, to act as peace maker if necessary, to summarize salient points, and to keep the group focused on the task at hand and moving toward the goal.

> **Treat each successive interview as if it were your first.**

Handling Several Formats

Some applicants will face a variety of interview types in the course of pursuing one position. Many candidates for a university faculty position, for example, encounter a series of interviews that span two days or more. Having flown or driven into town the night before, the next morning a member of the department will pick him up at his hotel. The morning may consist of several meetings: a meeting with the department chairperson, and meetings with two or three other faculty members as time and class schedules permit (**Series Interviews**). The candidate will go to lunch with several of the faculty (**Panel Interview**) and in the afternoon meet with the Dean of the Faculty and later successively with two or three additional faculty members (**Series Interviews**). During the evening a dinner meeting may be scheduled at the department chairperson's or a faculty member's home (**Panel and Series Interviews**). The next day consists of meetings with any faculty not seen individually on day one (**Series Interview**) and perhaps teaching a segment of a class (**Examination/Test Interview**). In the end, this individual will go through three or four different types of interviews and he will be judged by several people.

The most important thing to remember during series interviews is to treat each successive interview as if it were your first. Indeed, it is your first interview with this person. Try to be as alert, fresh, and dynamic with each person as you were with the very first one who interviewed you.

Interview Settings

Interviews can take place almost anywhere. The telephone screening interview will most likely take place with you in your home or office. At either place make sure you have your interview essentials ready and organized. If a **phone** call comes when you are at work, ask the interviewer to excuse you for a moment while you close the door. Take a moment to close the door, if this is possible, and to get your interview essentials out of your briefcase—or wherever you are keeping them. Take a deep breath to help calm you as you pick up the receiver to continue.

Face-to-face interviews most often take place in a hotel or college campus setting for screening interviews. Employment interviews usually take place in the employer's offices, but may occur at other sites. Some interviews, or at least parts of them, may take place in a restaurant, the employer's home, or even in an airport waiting area.

The portion of an interview that takes place in a restaurant can be the most dangerous minefield for many interviewees. Evening dinners in the employer's home often have the same effect. One potential problem is that many applicants who have been on their best behavior for the interviews in the more formal setting that preceded the **lunch or dinner** session now mistakenly believe that the interview is over and act accordingly!

As long as you are with the prospective employer or her representatives, the interview continues. The setting may change; the participants may seem to turn from talk of business related matters to a more social set of conversation topics; but you, the applicant, are still on stage and continue to be evaluated. This is no time to relax, let your hair down, and forget what you are there for. Continue to give thoughtful responses to questions and probe in a non-threatening manner for insight into the company where you may have the opportunity to work. Your interest and enthusiasm for the company must remain dynamic even if you are tired and worn out from travel and the stress of several series interviews.

Another consideration should be what you will order if you are in a restaurant and what you will take should you be eating in someone's home. If ordering from a menu, select something that will be easy to eat. Bony chicken or lobster in its shell are to be avoided along with spaghetti or anything else that may prove difficult to eat. You want to be able to give your full attention to your dinner companions and appear in control and well mannered rather than having to struggle with your food and only give half attention to your dinner companions.

If eating in someone's home, you will have fewer choices, but at least everyone else will be facing the same struggle you are if the host's menu choices have not been planned for ease of eating. However, you should still have some leeway. Take small portions of any foods you don't like or expect to be difficult to eat. You will probably find your appetite is not great and you probably won't be eating much today anyway. Eat enough to appear polite and keep you from starvation, but give your attention to your real purposes for being there—promote your candidacy and evaluate the position you hope will eventually be offered to you.

The question of alcoholic beverage consumption often arises as interviewees attempt to decide, "should I, or shouldn't I?" The best rule is to avoid completely any offer of alcohol at lunch. You need to be clear-headed for the interviews you are likely to still face that afternoon. And you do not want to give the impression that you may be one to drink at noon each day before

> **When ordering from a menu, select something that will be easy to eat.**

going back to the office for the afternoon's work, even though it may appear to be part of the work culture—or maybe it's just an interview test.

If you are at an evening dinner or cocktail party, you have some leeway with this rule. If you don't drink, simply decline the cocktail—there is no need for an explanation. If you do drink and wish to have a cocktail along with the others, then **one** is generally acceptable. No more tonight—no matter how many others may consume. If you are female, you may choose to ask for white wine. Many find this less objectionable for women than hard liquor. Some women may be offended by this advice, but now is the time to go after the job—not the inequities.

Questioning Techniques

Direct

Applicants encounter the direct questioning approach most frequently. Interviewers tend to use this method because it allows them to control the direction of the interview. Asking specific questions of each candidate is the questioning technique the majority of employers know best, and it allows them to feel the most comfortable. By asking similar questions of each candidate, interviewers find it easier to compare one applicant with another.

The interviewer who uses the direct questioning technique has specific questions and usually asks these in a planned sequence. Usually the interviewer asks questions that relate to your:

- Education
- Work experience
- Interpersonal skills
- Skills and strengths
- Ability to take initiative and solve problems
- Career goals

The direct questioning technique involves both open-ended and closed questions. Closed questions are those that can be answered with a simple "yes" or "no." Although candidates often will elaborate beyond the simple "yes" or "no," even these elaborations are usually more concise and to the point than answers to open-ended questions. Open-ended questions call for information, reflection, or judgment; they are intended to give the interviewer insights into the knowledge, personality, or character of the applicant. Open-ended questions must be answered with more than a "yes" or "no" and often begin with "what" or "how."

Indirect

The indirect interview technique is less structured than the direct method. It is also used less frequently than the direct method. When using this method, the interviewer wants you to talk as much as possible about yourself and the job so he or she can determine your likely performance as a result of this interview. The interviewer tends to ask broad general questions relating to several key areas that he thinks will elicit indicators of your likely on-the-job performance. Most questions are open-ended requiring elaboration from the interviewee. You might be asked, for example,

We had a problem last year with one employee who leaked information on our new product designs to our major competitor. What would you have done in this situation?

I see you have degrees in both engineering and sociology. That's an interesting combination. Tell me how your educational backgrounds in both fields might help you on this job.

We've talked about some of the challenges facing this office during the next two years. What would you want to accomplish during your first 90 days on the job? Could you give me some specific changes you would bring about immediately?

What kind of personality do you think would work best in this work environment?

Tell me more about your career goals over the next five to ten years and how they might relate to this job.

You may take several minutes responding to each question. And your response may lead the interviewer into related areas of questioning that were unplanned. It is this lack of planned structure as well as the lack of parallel questioning of other applicants that makes some employers uncomfortable and more likely to use the direct form of questioning.

In the indirect interview you will be at center stage doing most of the talking. You may feel more at ease during such an interview because you feel less pressure to come up with the "right answer" to specific questions. But beware of getting too comfortable; you are still being evaluated even though you are not answering a series of specific questions most commonly identified as the key to the interview process. The interviewer may be looking for key analytical, problem-solving, and communication skills along with determining your style, personality, and philosophies. In such a situation, **how** you answer the questions and converse with the interviewer may be just as important as **what** you say. Before responding, quickly try to determine what the interviewer is trying to assess. Try to focus your response and answer in an organized, coherent fashion. Be careful not to ramble in an unfocused stream of consciousness.

Stress

Although most interviews seem stressful to job applicants, fortunately for you, few interviewers actually put candidates through a **stress interview**. But since you could encounter one, you need to know what one is so you would recognize it and keep your composure if ever you are subjected to one.

Stress interviews may be conducted by one person or a panel of interviewers who fire numerous questions at the candidate. The interviewer's tone of voice may be threatening, and the questions which may be quickly fired at the applicant—like a barrage—may be accusatory in nature.

The purpose of a stress interview is to see how the applicant reacts in a stressful situation. Some employers use this method when interviewing for positions which require coping with on-the-job stress. A chief of campus security, for example, points out he always subjects potential officers to a stress interview. He's hard on them and his goal is to reduce an applicant—male or female—to tears. If he's successful however, the applicant is not hired. He wants people who can remain in control of themselves and stressful situations, and he believes the stress interview gives some indication of how well the candidate will perform under stress.

Not always is the connection between the stress interview and the stressful job as obvious as in the above case of the chief of security. But many employers want employees who can work in a pressure-filled atmosphere. While they can review the individual's record to learn how he or she has handled stress in the past, the stress interview gives some indication of how well the candidate will perform under stress.

If you encounter a stress interview, simply understanding what is happening and why should help you through the interview. Try to keep calm; take a deep breath and don't allow the interviewer to upset you; remain in control of yourself; and be complete but concise and to the point as you answer.

Examination/Testing

Some interviews will include elements of testing or examination. For some types of jobs, such as clerical or mechanical, you may be tested on the actual equipment you will be using. Teachers may be asked to conduct a one-hour classroom session where their performance will be observed and evaluated by both faculty and students. Certain questions, similar to those outlined in the section on indirect questions, may be asked to ascertain your level of knowledge, decision-making capabilities, analytic capabilities, and competence.

"What if" questions that begin with "What would you do if. . ."

are designed to test your ability to relate your past experience to the employer's current situation and needs. Using questions designed to test you, interviewers are looking for thoughtful answers that demonstrate your competence.

Interview Structure

Each interview will be different simply because the different combination of people involved and their goals produce different dynamics. However, there is a basic structure that approximates what one can expect in most interview situations. The actual conversation and amount of time spent in each phase will vary, but the progression from one phase to another will normally follow a predictable pattern. This structure is evident from the moment you arrive at the interview site to when you learn whether or not you were selected for the job.

Opening

As soon as you meet the interviewer, you normally spend some time in small talk. This gives both the employer and the applicant a chance to feel more at ease with each other and the situation. Discussions of the weather, whether the applicant had any trouble getting to the interview, and similar topics are usually briefly considered. The main goal of this exchange is to **establish rapport** between the interview participants.

Exchange Information

What we might refer to as the "body" of the interview is the phase that will normally have the most time devoted to it. It is now that the interviewer and interviewee will exchange information—with both persons posing questions as well as giving answers. The interviewer tries to size up the applicant in terms of his work abilities, level of knowledge, related experience, interpersonal skills, communication skills, motivation, dedication, loyalty, career goals, and likability. The interviewer attempts to give the applicant information about the position.

The applicant tries to make a favorable impression as he answers the questions posed by the interviewer and asks questions to probe the nature of the job.

Close

The close, like the opening, is another time for exchanging amenities. The employer will normally thank the applicant for coming, indicate she enjoyed meeting with him, and perhaps indicate that the company will be making a decision soon.

This is no time to murmur your thanks and meekly leave. This is your opportunity to refocus the interview toward your skills and how they fit the position as well as to determine what your next step should be. Briefly, try to summarize your strengths as they fit the position and employer's needs, indicate your appreciation for the time the interviewer has spent with you, but before you leave ask when you might expect to hear about their decision. (This could be an actual hiring decision or it may be a decision as to whom the company will invite back for further interviews.) Assuming you are given a time frame, ask the interviewer, it's perfectly acceptable to follow-up with this question:

> **This is no time to murmur your thanks and meekly leave.**

If I haven't heard anything by (select the date of the day following the date you were told a decision would be reached), may I call you to check on my status?

Usually the interviewer will say you may call. You now have a date by which you should follow-up if you have not heard about your hiring status.

Follow-Up

Later that same day, if possible, and no later than the following day, write a brief letter to the employer. This is a business letter, not a social thank you note. It should be typewritten on business size stationery and mailed in a business size envelope.

You can again thank the interviewer for the time she spent with you and indicate your continued interest in the position. You may choose to briefly restate your strengths as they relate to the position to be filled, and indicate that you look forward to hearing from her on (fill in the date she indicated they would have reached a hiring decision).

At the close of the interview you asked whether you could call the interviewer to check on your status if you hadn't heard by a certain date. When that date arrives, if you haven't heard—**CALL**. You have already set the stage for the call at the close of the interview, now follow-through.

You have nothing to gain by not making that call. By calling you let the interviewer know you are still interested and you have the tenacity to follow-through. If a decision hasn't been made, you may a score a few points in your favor. If a decision has been reached, and someone else has been offered the job, even if you are disappointed, you are better off knowing since you can now concentrate your efforts toward other positions. Thank the individual, and ask to be remembered for future openings they may have that would utilize your skills.

At this point you may even wish to write a final thank you letter indicating your continued interest in the firm and asking them to remember you for future openings in your line of work.

3

45 Key Interview Principles

Before formulating dynamite answers to interview questions, let's review some basic interview principles to prepare us for the job interview. If you understand interview goals—both your goals and the likely goals of the interviewer—and the process by which you both will attempt to reach these goals, you will be in a position to formulate your own dynamite answers to interview questions **and** better understand the ones we present to you to get you started.

Different Goals

Know that your goals and those of the interviewer will often differ. So it is important to understand the questions posed by the interviewer in terms of her goals—both the obvious goal and possible subtle "hidden agenda" type goals—as well as your own. At the most simplistic level, the interviewer wants to find the best person to fill the job opening. The best person is usually the one with:

- the most appropriate fit of skills, knowledge, and abilities to the position to be filled.

- the best fit with the company environment in terms of temperament.

- the best fit with any of the company's special needs such as someone who can travel, relocate, or put in long hours evenings or on weekends.

- an appropriate fit with the position in terms of salary history and expectations of salary and benefits.

Your goals are to ask the questions that will help you determine what the employer really is looking for, and whether you would want to work for this company or in this position at the same time that you are trying your best to convince the interviewer that you are the best person for the job! Not an easy feat.

Strategies For Interview Success

The principles that follow form the basis of strategies that should help you in any job interview. Some principles point you to necessary work to be done before you ever enter the interview situation. Other principles focus on concerns of the interviewer as her questions attempt to elicit answers that may tell her more than you wish if you are not thinking clearly as you respond. The final set of principles deal with actions you can take at the close of the interview as well as once it is over in order to maximize your chances of being offered the job.

Principles to Guide Interview Preparation

The job interview is much more than just answering a set of questions and preparing accordingly. It involves knowing about different types of interviews, various settings in which interviews take place, and a variety of interview formats and questioning techniques. You should prepare for all aspects of the interview by anticipating what lies ahead and how you should best present yourself both verbally and nonverbally.

1. Identify and assess your strengths.

One of the first steps any potential job seeker/job changer should take is to conduct a thorough-self assessment which consists of an evaluation of one's skills, abilities, and accomplishments. This is important in part so you will know what you are good at, but it is also a critical step toward being able to clearly communicate your strengths to potential employers. The old adage that you should "know thyself" is extremely important during all phases of your job search. With this self-knowledge you will be in a better position to tell employers what it is you do well, enjoy doing, and want to do in the future. This information will play an important role in both developing your resume and preparing for the interview. This self-assessment generates a useful language that stresses your major skills, abilities, and achievements.

2. Translate your strengths into job-related language of <u>accomplishments and benefits</u> relevant to the needs of employers.

It is one thing to say that you enjoy talking to people. But to tell an employer you enjoy speaking in front of groups and have a flair for holding their attention and getting the action you desire from them, translates your skill into a job-related benefit for the employer. Whenever possible, give **examples** of your strengths that relate to the language and needs of the employer.

> ## Stress <u>benefits</u> you are likely to provide for the employer.

3. Be sure to make your communications employer-centered rather than self-centered.

While you have specific needs in relation to the job—salary, benefits, satisfaction—these are self-centered interests which should not be the major issues discussed with interviewers. Always put yourself in the shoes of the interviewer—he or she has specific needs. Keep focused on what it is you can do for the employer rather than what the employer can do for you. Most of your answers and questions should stress **benefits** you are likely to provide for the employer. When preparing for the interview, be sure to use an employer-centered language of benefits.

4. Support your accomplishments with specific examples illustrating what you did.

Whenever you make a claim of your accomplishments, it will both be more believable and better remembered if you will cite specific examples or **supports** for your claims. Tell the interviewer something about a business related situation where you actually used this skill and elaborate about the outcome. If it actually occurred on the job, stress the benefits to the company where you were employed. Try to identify four or five good work-related examples of your accomplishments which you may be able to share with the interviewer. Avoid talking about "what happened" when you worked in another organization. Your story needs a subject—you—and an outcome—a benefit or performance.

5. Identify what you enjoy doing.

There are a lot of skills you may have honed to the point of excellence, but do you want to spend the better part of your work life engaging in this activity? When he was 95, George Burns claimed one reason he was still going strong and working a rather demanding schedule was that he loved his work! A secretary may have excellent typing skills but want to move up and out of consideration for another similar position. If this is the case, he doesn't want to stress his typing skill—even though he may be very good at it. Skills you really enjoy using are the ones you are most likely to continue to use to the benefit of both you and the employer.

6. Know about your "field of dreams" by conducting research on important job-related issues.

Before you go to your first job interview you should have conducted research on the field in which you plan to work. Though some of your information may come from printed materials and electronic source—reference materials in the library, company publications, or home pages on the

Internet—informational interviews with persons already working (or better yet hiring) in your field will yield information you will need later.

You want to know **before** you go for a job interview what range of salaries are offered in your geographical area for the kind of work you hope to do. Know what starting salaries are as well as the salary level for someone with your education and experience. Find out as much as you can about jobs **in general** in your field so that you can talk intelligently once you have a job interview. What are the duties and responsibilities? How far can one advance in this field? What kinds of special skills are useful? What training or degrees are required?

7. Gather information about the organization.

Prior to going to the interview, do your research on the organization. Find out as much as possible about what they do, their reputation, corporate goals, management philosophy, the kind of people they tend to hire, whether they primarily promote from within—any information you can gather will be to your advantage. It will help you make decisions about your desire to be a part of their team as well as ask better questions and give better responses to those they ask you in the course of the interview.

With large corporations much of this information is available in printed directories, such as the *Hoover Handbooks* and *Standard and Poors*, you can find in your local library and in promotional material—brochures and newsletters put out by the company. Many companies—both large and small—also maintain Web sites on the Internet They sites can provide a wealth of information on company operations, including directories of key personnel. You should supplement these printed and electronic resources by talking with people who work or have worked for the company. You can get a better assessment of interpersonal dynamics within an organization from talking with people. In the case of very small firms your only source of information may be talking with individuals in the community.

8. Gather information about the interviewer.

It is often said that organizations do not hire, people do. Thus it is to your advantage to try to find out what you can about the person(s) who will be conducting the interview as part of your data gathering on the organization. What is this person's background? What types of questions does he like to ask? What about his personality? Does he ask tough questions that put stress on interviewees? The more you know about that individual, the better you can phrase your responses in honest, but targeted, terms.

9. Talk in the employer's language.

Talk in the employer's language of organizational goals and expected performance. The employer is interested in getting the work done; getting it done in a timely manner; getting it done at a certain quality level; and getting it accomplished within budget. The employer is usually not interested in your career and personal goals except as they relate to your performance within the organization and the company's "bottom line."

10. Anticipate and prepare for questions.

You can anticipate before you ever walk into the interview 90%-95% of the questions you will be asked. You can expect to be asked about your education and work experience as they relate to the job under consideration. You may be asked questions about your personality, work habits, ability to work with others, or your career goals. In addition to the standard areas of inquiry, a look at your resume should tell you if there are areas likely to get the attention of the interviewer. Do you have unexplained time gaps in your education or work life? Have you jumped around from employer to employer in a short time period? Are you applying for a position that is significantly below your apparent abilities and previous work experience?

In other words, if there is anything that is likely to have come to the attention of the interviewer as questionable—either positive or negative—expect that you will be asked about it during the interview and prepare accordingly. It is far easier to think how you would respond in an honest, yet positive manner to a question when you are in the relatively comfortable surroundings of home than in the midst of a stressful interview.

Gather the information necessary to respond intelligently to the questions you are likely to be asked, collect your thoughts, and plan strategies for responding to various likely lines of questioning.

11. Consider your response if asked an illegal question.

We are happy to report that the incidence of employers asking illegal questions of an interviewee has declined significantly since the early days of affirmative action. However, it can still happen. Consider prior to the interview how you would respond if you were to be asked an illegal question or one inappropriate for the work setting or unrelated to the job requirements.

Your options are to inform the interviewer it is an illegal question and you will not answer it; tactfully indicate that since the question deals with an area of illegal inquiry, are they sure they want you to respond to it; indicate tactfully that although an illegal area of inquiry, you welcome the chance to respond to it; ask how the question relates to the job for which you are interviewing; or you may choose to answer the question. Choose an option with which you feel comfortable in terms of both your response as well as the likely impact it may have on a job offer.

12. Practice the form and content of your responses.

Most people find it is good preparation to practice various responses to anticipated questions. This does not mean that you try to memorize answers—whether someone else's or your own—but rather that after thinking through the basic strategy to your response, you try to actually verbalize an answer. Most people find it useful to go through this process several times prior to an interview.

13. Practice questions with a friend or tape recorder.

Preparing for the interview in isolation of feedback information for evaluating your potential performance is likely to produce less than satisfactory results. Try to enlist a friend to help you prepare for the interview. You may want to role play—your friend becomes the interviewer and you the interviewee. Run through a practice interview session where you must do everything from greet the interviewer to answer specific questions and close the interview. Tape record your answers to questions and analyze them to see if you indeed stress your strengths and benefits to the interviewer. Do you provide examples and supports? Are your answers always positive in content? Are you employer-centered? Keep practicing until you're comfortable in answering/asking questions.

14. Be prepared for different types and settings of interviews.

You should be prepared for two types of interviews: informational/networking and employment. These may occur over the telephone or in face-to-face settings such as the employer's office, a restaurant, or in a social setting. If, for example, you are interviewed in a restaurant, be sure you observe proper eating etiquette as well as avoid ordering foods that can be difficult to eat, such as spaghetti or crabs. Your eating behavior will be observed. How and what you eat may be as important to the interview as how you answer the questions. And don't answer questions with a mouth full of food!

15. Be prepared for more than one interview with the same employer.

Many interviewees are surprised to learn they are subjected to more than one interview with the same employer. They normally experience two interviews: screening and hiring/placement. The screening interview may take place over the telephone. Here, you must be prepared for that unexpected telephone call in which the employer probes about your continuing interest in the position, your availability, and your job-related expectations, including perhaps salary requirements. The hiring/placement interview is normally conducted in the interviewer's office. But it may involve a one-to-one interview or sequential, series, panel, or group interviews. This process could take place over a one or two week period in which you are called back to meet with other individuals in one-to-one, series, panel, or group interview situations. Each interview may probe a different level of your interests, abilities, knowledge, and skills.

16. Be prepared for different questioning techniques.

While you may be prepared to answer direct questions with direct answers, some interviewers also include indirect and stress questioning techniques. For example, rather than ask you "Do you have difficulty working with your employers," they may ask "Why did you leave your last three jobs?" or "How did you get along with your last three employers?" Rather than ask you directly about your social status and financial situation, they may ask you "Where do you prefer living in the community?" If a job involves a great deal of stress, the interviewer may ask you questions that put you under stress during the interview just to see how you handle such situations. For example, you may unexpectedly be asked "If we hire you and three months later decide you're not the person we want, what are we going to do?" or "We normally don't hire someone without a college degree. Do you plan to complete college?" You may very well be thrown questions that are designed to challenge what may be perceived to be your well-rehearsed interview script. Remember, interviewers will be looking for indications of your weaknesses by asking questions that elicit such indicators.

17. Know how you communicate verbally to others.

Strong verbal communication skills are highly valued by most employers. They are signs of educated and competent individuals. Do you, for example, speak in complete and intelligible sentences? How's your diction? Do you say "going" rather than "goin," "going to" rather than "gonna," "didn't" rather than "din't," "yes" rather than "yea." Do you have a tendency to use vocalized phases ("ahs" and "uhms") and fillers ("you know," "like," "okay"). How's your grammar? Do you use the active rather than passive voice? Do you avoid using tentative, indecisive terms, such as "I think," "I guess," "I feel." Do you avoid ambiguous and negative terms such as "pretty good" or "fairly well" which say little if anything; they may even communicate negatives—that what you did was not good!

18. Know how you communicate nonverbally to others.

How do you dress, groom, greet others, shake hands, use eye contact, sit in a chair or on a sofa, maintain posture, use your hands, move your head, maintain facial expressions, listen positively, eat, drink, or enter and leave a room? These are nonverbal behaviors that may say more about your competence and personality than what you say in the interview. You may want to videotape yourself in a mock interview setting to see how you communicate both verbally and nonverbally.

19. Dress for success.

Before you ever open your mouth to speak, your appearance has already made an impression. Since you never get a second chance to make a first impression, make it a good one. Make the first few seconds of the interview work for you by nonverbally communicating your class, professionalism, and competence.

20. Prepare your telephone area.

Once you have made known your job search intentions—whether by sending out resumes, networking, or conducting informational interviews—you may receive a telephone call from an employer quite unexpectedly. It may be a call to schedule an interview, but most likely it will incorporate a "screening interview."

Be prepared by keeping essential items related to this potential telephone interview in an area by the phone. Minimum supplies should include a pad of paper, pen, copy of your resume, and note cards or equivalent on which you have information on all the companies which you have contacted as part of your job search.

Principles to Guide the Interview Encounter

Many of the principles identified for interview preparation are also principles applied to the interview encounter. Others, however, specifically relate to the interview process. The following 22 principles will help you get through the job interview.

21. Arrive on time.

There's nothing worse than to arrive late for a job interview. Since the first five minutes of the interview are the most important, arrive five minutes late and you effectively kill much of the interview—and your chances of getting the job. Your tardiness will be remembered and in a negative light. Always try to arrive at least 10 minutes early. If need be, drive to the interview site the day before to estimate how long it will take you to get there as well as find parking. Allow plenty of time, anticipating that you could well lose a half hour or more to bad traffic.

22. Treat everyone you meet as important to interview.

When you initially arrive at the interview site, chances are you will enter a reception area, meet a receptionist or secretary, and be asked to sit in this waiting area. Other employees also may enter this area while you are waiting. Make sure you are courteous to the receptionist or secretary or anyone else you meet. Also, you should appear competent in how you greet these people, sit, and what you read. For example, you should greet the receptionist or secretary by introducing yourself: "Good morning. I'm Jane Morris. I have a 9 o'clock appointment with Mr. Jameson." Wait to be invited to sit in a specific place. If you are wearing an overcoat, take it off before sitting. Interviewers sometimes ask these employees for their reaction to candidates: "What did you think about the candidate? Did you have a chance to talk to her? What did she do while she was waiting to meet me? Do you think you'll like her?" The opinions of such people can be very important to the interview process. So make sure you treat everyone you meet as **important** to the interview.

23. When waiting for the interviewer, do something that looks relevant to the interview and job.

While waiting to meet the interviewer, do something that looks relevant to the organization and interview. For example, you might engage the receptionist or secretary in small talk concerning the organization, employees, and the interviewer. Try to learn something relevant to the interview. You might ask some of these questions: "How many employees work here? How long have you been with the organization? Has Mr. Jameson been with this company long? What did he do before moving to this position? How do most people like working here? What computer system do you use?" Don't overdo it by becoming an interrogator or asking self-centered questions, such as questions about parking privileges, vacation time, benefits, or office space. Your small talk should emphasize your interest in the organization as well as generate information about the organization and interviewer relevant to the interview. You might learn something important that will help initiate small talk with the interviewer or raise a question you feel needs to be answered. Might you want to raise certain questions with the interviewer if you where told in the lobby that there's a lot of stress in the organization, many employees have left during the past six months, or not many people stay around here more than two years? That's important inside information indicative of possible internal political and management problems you may want to question. It's best to learn this now rather than become a victim of company stress or Byzantine politics.

24. Greet the interviewer properly.

Chances are the interviewer will come out to the reception area to greet you. Stand up straight, shake hands firmly, maintain eye contact, listen carefully, look energetic, speak in the positive, and introduce yourself: "Hello, I'm Jane Morris. It's a pleasure to meet you." Watch the small talk carefully. This is not a time to tell dumb jokes, look tired, or appear nervous. If you are asked if you had any trouble finding the place or parking your car, appear competent and positive by indicating you handled this part of the interview with ease.

25. Communicate positive behaviors during the critical first five minutes.

The first five minutes of the interview, which may not even address job-related questions, are the most important to the interview. It's during this time that critical first impressions are made and interviewers decide whether or not they like you. And being likable is one of the most important criterion for being selected for a job. If you make an excellent first impression—from shaking hands and dressing right to handling the initial small talk—the rest of the interview may go extremely well as the interviewer helps you through the interview. He or she may have decided during the third minute that you should be hired. The questions and answers may merely reinforce these initial impressions. Make sure your perfume or cologne is applied in moderate amounts and jewelry has been minimized. You don't want to be remembered for your strong scent or the noise your clanging jewelry generated! Indeed, many interviewers smell their interviewee as they pass in front of them when entering the interviewer's room.

26. Wait to be invited to sit in a particular seat rather than find your own place.

The particular seating arrangement for the interview may be important to the interviewer. You may, for example, be asked to sit on the other side of a desk or table. Alternatively, you may be invited to sit on a sofa. Whatever the case, don't look like you are in a hurry by taking a seat before you are invited to sit. Chances are you will be seated within six feet of the interviewer—a comfortable conversational distance that enables both of you to maintain good eye contact.

27. Keep your hands, arms, and elbows to yourself.

If you are sitting at a desk, keep your hands, arms, and elbows off the desk and away from any distracting items such as pencils or pens. Try to look alert, energetic, and focused on the interviewer rather than fidget with items that indicate your nervousness or irritating habits. If you don't know what to do with your hands, try folding or steepling them.

28. Sit erect and lean slightly forward.

Avoid leaning back in your chair or on the sofa looking extremely comfortable and relaxed. Such posture may communicate that you are more interested in talking about yourself than in listening to and learning from the interviewer. The best sitting posture is to sit erect and lean slightly forward toward the interviewer folding or steepling your hands. This is good listening posture. Nonverbally it communicates that you are interested in the individual. You will look more alert and energetic in this posture than in other postures.

> **The most important impressions are made during the first five minutes.**

29. Keep your feet on the floor.

If you are sitting on a sofa where your full body is in view, avoid crossing your legs and showing the soles of your shoes. Keep both feet on the floor. Crossed legs still indicate a degree of informality and familiarity that is unwarranted at this point in your relationship with the interviewer.

30. Let the interviewer initiate the openers but take initiative in offering some of your own openers.

It is the responsibility of the interviewer to initiate openers. During the first two or three minutes the interviewer will probably talk about your trip to the office, the weather, your impressions of the facilities, or some other small talk topics. Respond to these questions with more than just "yes" or "no" answers and observations. You need to take some initiative here to express your personality. Initiate your own positive small talk by making an interesting observation about the office, such as the art work or decorating, or the personnel you met in the reception area. You might, for example, discover from seeing a framed degree hanging on the wall that the interviewer is a graduate of your alma mater. He or she may be a collector of unusual items that are displayed in the office. Or he or she may have an interesting photo displayed of family, friends, colleagues, a ceremony, or someone famous. Show some personal interest in the individual by focusing on one or two items for small talk. This small talk period may result in building

> **Small talk means developing a conversational line that has a purpose and establishes an agenda.**

an important **personal bridge** between you and the interviewer that will make this professional encounter a much easier and more enjoyable one. Remember, the most important impressions are made during the first five minutes. You want to appear energetic, positive, and interesting during these initial moments of the interview. In the end, how you handle yourself in the small talk may be more important to getting the job than how you handle yourself with the standard interview questions.

31. Be prepared to respond to initial small talk in an interesting and positive manner.

Small talk does count! It indicates something about your social capabilities which may be just as important to the job as your work-content skills. Small talk does not mean telling jokes. It means developing a conversational line that has a purpose and establishes an agenda. If you need assistance on developing your small talk skills, we recommend two excellent books on this subject: Anne Baber and Lynne Waymon, *Great Connections: Small Talk and Networking For Businesspeople* and Susan RoAne, *How to Work a Room*. Both books are available directly from Impact Publications by completing the order form at the end of this book.

32. Answer questions with complete sentences and with substance.

Avoid simple "yes" or "no" answers. Remember, the interviewer is looking for **indicators of substance and benefits**. Answers which are too brief give him little information about you. They may indicate a lack of interest or substance on your part. The interviewer should leave this interview saying "I feel good about this person. He gave good answers to my questions." If you don't answer the questions completely, how can this person feel good about you?

33. Reduce your nervousness by practicing a few stress reduction techniques.

You can better control your nervousness by following the same advice often given to public speakers. As you walk into the interview room, try to take slow deep breaths. You can do this subtly so the interviewer will be unaware of it. And although this is easier said than done, the more you can get your mind off yourself and concentrate on the other person, the more comfortable you will feel. If you are nervous, you are probably focusing too much attention on yourself. You are self-consciously concerned with how you are doing and what impression you are making on others. Try to be more other-directed. Rather than concentrate on your needs and fears, concern yourself with the employer's needs and questions. Preparation is probably the greatest aid in lessening nervousness. If you followed Principles 1-20 and arrived on time (Principle 21), you should walk into the interview feeling well prepared and confident. If you arrive early for the interview, you will have a chance to collect your thoughts, take those deep breaths, and focus your attention toward the employer.

> **If you are nervous, you are probably focusing too much attention on yourself.**

34. Focus on the interviewer's needs.

Assume that most interviewers need to select someone who will fit into their organization well in terms of both productivity and personality. You must confirm during the interview that you are both a productive and personable individual. You do this by stressing your benefits for the employer and handling well the questions and small talk so that in the end you will be evaluated in the most positive manner possible.

35. Orient yourself toward exchanging useful information about each other rather than just on getting the job.

Keep in mind your objectives and goals. Remember, both you and the interviewer need to acquire information that will best assist each other in arriving at a proper decision. If you focus all your answers and questions on making a "good impression" so you can get the job, you will probably be very nervous and make mistakes along the way. Take it easy and focus on what you should really be doing—getting and gathering information that can be used for making a decision. In your case, you need information on the job, employer, and organization. Is this really the place you want to work? Will it be right for you? The employer also has similar questions about you.

36. Emphasize the positive.

You want both the content of your responses and the manner in which you phrase your answers to be positive.

As you talk about your previous employer(s), try to cast them in as positive a view as possible. After all, if an interviewee talks negatively about a former employer, as an employer I assume someday he'll talk that way about me. If he bad-mouths his former company, I expect that one day he'll do the same to mine. If he has only negative remarks about his co-workers, I must question his ability to get along in my organization as well. In other words, you have little to gain—and much to lose—with this person by venting frustrations about previous jobs.

Try to put on the most positive "spin" possible— honest,

but not stupid—as you phrase your responses. Avoid negative words like "can't," "didn't," "wouldn't," and phrase your answers with positive words instead. Rather than say, "I wouldn't want to travel more than 4-5 days per month," you could respond with a more positive, "I would prefer to keep my travel to 4-5 days per month." Practice being more positive in your day-to-day communication and you will find it will come to you more easily in an interview.

37. Turn potential negatives into positives.

While interviewers also want to know what's wrong about you—your negatives—you want to continuously stress your positives—what's right about you. You can do this by maintaining a positive orientation toward all questions.

Most applicants, for example, have some qualification or lack of a qualification that they, as well as potential employers, may consider to be a negative which is likely to knock them out of consideration for the position. Perhaps you are just out of school and hence don't have experience. Maybe you are over 50 and, although you know it is illegal for an employer to discriminate against you on the basis of your age, you believe this will be a hindrance to your getting a job. Perhaps you have not stayed in your past jobs for very long and your resume shows a pattern of job-hopping. Maybe your grades in school were average at best.

Whatever the negatives you believe will hinder your efforts at landing a job, you should attempt to find a way to turn the negative into an honest positive. Caryl recalls an older woman—over 65—who came into her office where she was the personnel director several years ago. The woman evidently thought her age would be a negative, so she came prepared with several advantages to hiring someone her age. Her first advantage was that she "would not get pregnant!"

38. Engage in positive nonverbal cues.

Studies of the employment process indicate that 65-70% of a hiring decision may be based on nonverbal communication. Nonverbal messages—your appearance and dress —are the first to be communicated to an interviewer. The enthusiasm in your voice and animation in your face indicate your interest in the job as well as suggest an energy level conducive to getting things done. Your eye contact with the interviewer helps establish rapport and maintain interest. Because nonverbal messages are much harder to control, people tend to believe nonverbal messages over verbal ones. So make your nonverbal communication work for you. Pay particular attention to your dress, accessories, make-up, scent, hand shake, facial expressions, eye contact, sitting, and listening behaviors.

39. Be sure to ask questions.

Be prepared to ask several questions relevant to the job, employer, and organization. These questions should be designed to elicit information to help you make a decision as well as demonstrate your interest, intelligence, and enthusiasm for the job. You may want to write out several of these questions on a 3x5"card to help you remember the questions you want to ask. It's okay to refer to the card during the interview. Just mention to the interviewer that "I have a few questions I wanted to ask you. I made some notes so I would be sure to ask them." Then take out your notes and ask the questions. This indicates to the interviewer that you are prepared and have specific concerns he or she must also address. We outline several of these questions in Chapter 7. However, avoid asking questions about salary and benefits. These questions are too self-centered at this point. They are best left to the very end—once you receive a job offer and begin negotiating your terms of employment.

40. Delay salary considerations as long as possible.

Usually salary is brought up by the interviewer either near the end of the first interview or after a job offer has been made. However, some interviewers will bring it up earlier. It is almost always to your advantage to delay discussion of salary as long as possible. In the meantime, you need to do two things:

- Determine the **worth** of the position.
- Demonstrate your **value** to the employer.

You can only do these two things **after** you have had a chance to interview for the position—not at the beginning or in the middle of the interview. You need to have the opportunity to determine what the job is worth based on the duties and responsibilities of the position—something you can best evaluate after you have a chance to ask questions about the position. You also want the opportunity to promote your value to the employer which you have a chance to demonstrate and support during the give and take of the interview.

Interviewers who bring up salary early—during a telephone screening interview or early in the initial interview—are usually trying to screen people out of consideration based on salary expectations that are either too high or even too low! Attempt to stall by indicating that salary is "open" or that you need to know more about the position before you can discuss salary.

41. Delay accepting an offer until you can consider it.

Once you are offered the job, your immediate response may be to accept it right there on the spot. In most cases you are better off to request a day or two to consider the offer. This gives you a chance to weigh whether you really want this job; check your status at any other organizations where you have applied for a position; and perhaps to even negotiate a better employment package either with this employer or at one of the other firms who may decide if they want you they will have to act now.

It is reasonable to ask for 24-48 hours to consider the offer as well as discuss it with other family members.

42. Close by asking when to follow-up.

At the end of the interview make sure you know what the next step is—further interviews or an employment decision—and when the employer expects to make a decision. Once she indicates a hiring decision date, ask if you may call a day or two after that date if you have not yet heard. If she says they expect to make a decision by the 10th, ask,

"If I haven't heard anything by the 12th, may I call you to check my status?" In most cases you will be given an okay to call.

Now you know the date by which you should start calling, and it will be easier for you to place the call since you have provided the entre.

After the Interview—Follow-Up

The interview is not over when you shake hands and leave the interview site. It's over when you get and accept the job offer or another applicant is hired. Therefore, plan to do additional things during the post interview period to enhance your candidacy.

43. Record information about the interview for future reference.

Often you will have more than one interview—probably a series—with a company. Make notes while the interview is fresh in your mind within 24-hours after you leave the interview. Include the name and position of the interviewer(s), information about the job (duties, salary)—anything pertinent to the position, your qualifications for the position which you stressed in the interview, and any other information you may need later.

You will have a summary of the interview which you can review prior to a future interview with the firm—whether a follow-up interview for this same position or another opening at a later time.

44. Send a thank you letter.

As soon as possible following the interview—later the same day or the next day at the latest—send a thank you letter. In this letter express your appreciation for the time the interviewer(s) spent with you, indicate your continued interest in the position (if this is the case), and restate any special skills or experience you would bring to the job (keep this brief and well focused.)

This is a business letter and the stationary, format, and method of writing—typewriter or letter quality printer—should reflect this.

45. Follow through with a telephone call when the decision date has passed.

Remember when at the end of the interview you asked when a decision would be made, and asked whether you could call if you hadn't heard within a couple of days of that date? Don't just ask the question and leave it at that—you must follow through. If the decision date has passed you must make the follow-up call.

If no decision has yet been made your call will remind them of your continued interest. You also should impress the employer as someone who does follow through, and he could expect this same commitment from you as an employee. If the employer has made a decision and was about to call and offer you the position, that's great! If someone else has been offered the job you may be disappointed, but it is just as well to find out now and concentrate your job search efforts elsewhere than to waste your time waiting to hear about this job.

If you put all of these interview principles into practice, you will be in an excellent position to get the job. You will approach the interview with confidence, energy, and enthusiasm. You will impress the interviewer as someone she would like to have working in the organization.

Let us now turn our attention to applying these principles to each step in the interview process, from preparation to follow-up. The following chapters elaborate on many of these previous principles. They address the many questions you are likely to encounter in interview situations as well as the questions you should ask during the interview.

4

Dynamite Preparation

Ne of the best ways to lower your stress level and avoid those sweaty palms and wobbly knees as you face a job interview is to prepare well. Knowing you are well prepared, your self confidence will soar. You'll be better able to concentrate on communicating your strengths to the employer rather than merely trying to impress the interviewer with "the right" answers to questions. You will feel better about yourself, and you will do better in the interview. Thorough preparation takes time and involves some practice, but it is a critical step to a dynamite interview.

This is no substitute for solid preparation. Don't risk interview failure by attempting to take shortcuts and assuming that because you are glib you will "wing-it" when you get to the interview. You may be able to fill silent spaces with talk, but your responses will most likely lack coherency and focus. Overall, without preparation, most people engage in what could best be termed "a stream of consciousness" and appear disorganized and inept.

Prepare For the Interview

The principles for interview preparation in Chapter 3 provide guidance for much of what you need to do as you gear up for job interviews. To get a better understanding of what's involved here, let's begin by dividing interview preparation principles into five categories:

- Assess your strengths and relate them to employers needs.

- Conduct research on the field of work you hope to enter as well as conduct research on organizations in your targeted community that hire for these types of positions.

- Prepare for the verbal interchange.

- Prepare your non-verbal strategies.

- Deal with logistics.

Preparation takes time, but since your livelihood as well as your work satisfaction and enjoyment of the work you do are on the line, it is time well spent.

Assess Strengths and Relate to Employer's Needs

If you have not already done so, you should assess your work related strengths and consider ways to relate these to the employer's needs. Principles 1-5 in the previous chapter deal with this process. Before you talk to an employer—in fact, before you even write your resume—you should have a clear understanding of what you do well and enjoy doing. What are your major skills? How have you demonstrated them in your past work? Can you elaborate your seven major achievements and relate them to the needs of the employer? What are your major weaknesses? Remember, employers are interested in hiring your strengths—those things you do well and enjoy doing. They will be looking for indicators of your weaknesses in the way you answer questions. Some may even ask you the question "What are some of your weaknesses?" From the very beginning of your job search, you should have identified your strengths and communicated them clearly to employers in your resumes, letters, and networking activities. The job interview enables you to further communicate your strengths to the employer. But you will only be able to do so if you first conduct a thorough assessment of what you do

> **Employers are interested in hiring your strengths.**

well and enjoy doing. Don't begin looking for a job until you first complete this self assessment. For more information on self assessment, see another of our books, *Discover the Best Jobs For You*.

Research Your Field of Work and Related Organizations

You need to gather as much information as possible about your industry in general and your field of work in particular. You should also find out as much as you can about the organizations in your targeted community—this may be where you live or where you would like to live—that hire for the kinds of positions in which you have interest. Principles 6-8 in Chapter 3 discuss this process.

If you are interested in working for a large corporation you will be able to obtain some information from **written sources**—business directories available in the reference section of your local library as well as public relations brochures you can obtain from the company. If you are interested in working for a small local firm there will be less available in printed publications, but this does not preclude you from doing research. Check the Internet. Most firms, regardless of size, have Web sites that offer a great deal of information about the organization.

Whether you are researching a small local firm or a huge multinational corporation, information gathered by **talking with people** who are familiar with the company will likely yield the most useful information. Do you know someone who works for the company or who has worked for the company recently? These are important people to talk with. If you don't know anyone who is or has been an employee, ask your friends if any of them do. Put the word out that you are interested in finding out more about the company. Chances are someone you know will know of someone who can answer many of your questions. These personal contacts will provide insights not normally available in printed company publications or in business directories.

Finally, don't overlook the opportunity to conduct **informational interviews**. An informational interview is one that you initiate with someone within an organization for the purpose of gathering information about a specific field or a type of job. Your goal is to get information that will be helpful to you in further clarifying your job goals, determining any additional training you may need to qualify, identifying organizations that provide employment opportunities in this particular arena, assessing whether the type of work is something you will be interested in doing on a daily basis, determining whether it is a growth field that will continue to provide employment opportunities as well as career advancement, and gathering salary information for various levels within the field.

The information gleaned from this type of interview can help you make career choices, make contacts within the field that may be useful to you later, and provide information on industry salary ranges that should be useful in employment interviews when the salary question is discussed.

Remember though, that at no time during an informational interview should you ask for a job. This is an infringement on the good graces of the employer who agreed to take time out of a busy schedule to help you. To ask about a job in this situation will get you remembered, but not in the positive way you would like. For more information on conducting informational interviews see two of our other books, ***Dynamite Networking For Dynamite Jobs*** and ***Interview For Success***.

Once you have a job interview scheduled, use your contacts—friends who are familiar with the company or persons with whom you conducted informational interviews, if appropriate—to fill in any gaps in your information as well as to try to get information about the person(s) who will be conducting your interview.

Prepare For the Verbal Interchange

To prepare for the verbal interchange, consider principles 9-17 in the previous chapter. You need to be able to talk the employer's language. Though you are advised to keep jargon to a minimum if your interview is being conducted by someone from personnel, use of limited jargon of the industry can be a plus if you are interviewed by the head of the operating unit. You don't want to overdo it, but some familiarity with the jargon appropriate to the position and industry identifies you as an insider.

Speaking the employer's language includes acknowledging a commitment to common goals which may include producing a high quality product, maintaining an efficiently run department, achieving cost cutting targets, increasing sales, or improving profits. Your knowledge of the industry, the company, and even the interviewer—which you have already researched—should help you identify the goals appropriate to this employer's situation.

You need to anticipate and prepare for the kinds of questions you are most likely to be asked. You do not need to be a mind reader or have powers of clairvoyance to do this. Just as the President can anticipate the likely areas of questioning he will encounter at a press conference and prepare accordingly, you too can identify the kinds of questions you are most likely to be asked.

The most common areas of questioning for job interviews tend to deal with your education, work experience, interpersonal skills—ability to work with others, follow directions of others, as well as take a leadership role when the situation warrants. Personality considerations include questions dealing with how well you work under pressure, whether you take initiative, or assume responsibility are important for many positions. Your answers to questions relating to your career goals—whether you will be happy in a position that may not allow for rapid advancement, your level of dedication to your work (will you put in long hours when necessary?), and how loyal you will be to your employer—are of concern to many employers. You can expect questions—direct or indirect—to be posed in an attempt to assess how you would fit into the job as well as the organization.

Some organizations prize individualism and a sense of entrepreneurship in their employers. They want individuals who are willing to take initiative and a certain amount of calculated risk. However, in other organizations such personal characteristics would likely lead to dismissal. Both you and the employer should be attempting to assess the "fit" between your goals and skills and the organization's goals and needs. If the fit is there, fine. You need to focus on the areas of fit. However, if it doesn't seem to be a good match, it may be to both your and the employer's benefit to find that out now. It will save you both a lot of headaches and probably expense later.

If there is anything that stands out on your resume or application—anything that sets you apart whether potentially a positive or negative—you can expect you will be asked about that. Again, you anticipate the line of questioning and think through possible responses. You want to consider how this is likely to be viewed by the employer and then what your strongest response—honest, but not stupid—would be.

Most people find it useful to practice an interview. This can be done with a spouse or friend, but if you know someone who conducts hiring interviews as part of their job, you may want to ask them to help you through a practice session. By talking through your responses to at least some of the questions you expect to be asked, you both get a sense of the areas of questioning where you need to reconsider your strategy as well as gain confidence in the areas where you feel good about your answers. The more times you can engage in practice sessions—ideally with different people conducting the interview—the more confident you are likely to feel.

You also might want to tape record your answers to possible questions. Listen carefully to how you answer each question. Do your answers conform to our principles of verbal communication in Chapter 3, especially using good grammar and avoiding vocalized pauses and fillers? If you use a tape recorder, you will get direct feedback on your verbal performance. You will be able to compare your responses for evidence of improvement.

As you practice, however, keep in mind that you do **not** want to give memorized or "canned" responses to questions. You are developing strategies for formulating types of responses for communicating certain ideas. You should not be concerned with replicating the actual words you use to communicate these ideas since the words you use will be somewhat different each time you respond. You want to become comfortable with the thrust of the message you want to convey, but you do not try to say it the same way each time. The response itself must remain spontaneous. If you answer employer's questions with what sound like prepared, memorized answers, you will not make a positive impression on the interviewer.

Though your preparatory research has answered many questions you may have initially had about jobs in your field as well as the hiring organizations, you will no doubt have more specific questions as you get ready for the job interview. Prepare a list of questions you want to ask the interviewer. Write them out neatly and carry this list with you to the interview. No doubt many of the questions will be answered in the course of the inter-

> You do **not** want to give memorized or "canned" responses to questions.

view, but you may forget some of them under the stress of the moment. When you feel you are nearing the close of the interview, or if the interviewer asks whether you have any other questions, take out your list and quickly scan it to see what areas, if any, have not yet been covered. If all have been covered, that's fine; you can indicate this to the employer. If there are some you still need to ask, this is your opportunity. Either way, you appear prepared and it is obvious you have given some thought to information you need from the employer. The interviewer should view this type of preparation in a positive light.

You should be prepared for encountering different types of interviews, settings and questioning techniques from your reading of our second chapter.

Nonverbal Elements of Success

So much is written about the verbal interchange that applicants sometimes forget that their nonverbal behavior may communicate at least as much to an employer as what they say. Principles 18-19 in the previous chapter deal with nonverbal communication. Some studies indicate that approximately two-thirds of a message is communicated nonverbally, so it is an important aspect of any interview.

Planning how you will dress for your interview is an important aspect of interview preparation—one that can further or sabotage your interview goals. Chapter 6 will deal with proper attire to promote your interview goals along with other ways to promote yourself nonverbally.

Deal With Logistics

There are many details that can make or break how well you present yourself to employers. The final preparation principle in Chapter 3 dealt with preparing your telephone area so that you would be ready to handle an unexpected screening interview. Having the essentials ready by your phone so you can respond to questions or schedule an interview will help you create a positive impression.

Once you have an interview scheduled, make certain you know where it is to be held, how to get there, and how long it will take to get there at the time of day you will be going. You may even wish to make a "practice run" in order to assure yourself that there will no surprises the day of the interview.

Try to get a good night's sleep the night before your interview. Do your preparing ahead of time and get to bed at a decent hour so you will be rested and can think clearly. Eat lightly—whether it be breakfast or lunch—prior to your interview. You probably won't be very hungry anyway. By eating lightly your energy can be focused on the interview rather than used in the process of digesting food.

Avoid alcohol. It won't calm your nerves, and it won't help you answer questions better—you'll just think you have!

5

Dynamite Answers: The Verbal Interchange

Most of your attention will be focused on answering specific questions raised by the interviewer. In preparation for these questions, you need to know what questions are most likely to be asked and how you should best formulate answers for greatest impact. Keep in mind that the interviewer is looking for indicators of your expertise, competence, motivation, interpersonal skills, decision-making skills, interest in job, personality, and likability. You will express many of these qualities when you answer the many questions posed by the interviewer. He will look for verbal clues of both your strengths and your weaknesses.

Interview Phases

Your verbal encounter with the interviewer will most likely pass through several distinct interview phases. Most interviewers will more or less sequence the interview into the following seven phases:

1. Greeting
2. Establishing common ground/icebreakers.
3. Indicating purpose of interview.
4. Drawing out information through the exchange of questions and answers:
   - General and specific questions
   - Brief and drawn out answers
   - Conversations to clarify questions, explain answers, and reach mutual understanding
5. Summarizing information and understanding.
6. Indicating next steps to be taken.
7. Closing.

The interviewer will be prepared with different types of questions and comments for each interview phase. You should be prepared to respond positively to each of these phases.

Expect the greeting to be short. It will go something like this. The interviewer will extend her hand and say

> How do you do Mr. Anthony. I'm Sarah White. Glad you could come in this morning.

The next thing that usually happens—just before the interviewer explains the purpose for the interview—is that you engage in a few minutes of small talk. This brief period gives both of you a chance to feel more at ease with each other. If you know something about the interviewer's interests—either from information gathered in your research or because of something you see in the office—you might use this topic to establish common ground.

Small talk for establishing common ground is important. For

example, we know a young women who applied for a teaching position at a community college. A few weeks earlier, she had read Mager's book on behavioral objectives for instruction. At the beginning of the interview, she noticed a copy of Mager's book lying on the interviewer's desk and commented about it. The interviewer was pleased to learn she was familiar with it. She is convinced to this day that it was a major factor in getting the job offer. It established common ground and set her apart from the many other people applying for the same position.

You might, for example, notice a photo, framed degree, award plaque, or an office decoration that may become the center for small talk. The topic might lead to establishing common ground through an interesting small talk conversation. You might comment that you noticed the framed degree from XYZ University. Perhaps you know someone who also graduated from there and by chance the interviewer also knows that person. Maybe you know something about the scholastic excellence or outstanding athletic program of the institution. A comment about an award plaque could lead to an interesting conversation about the interviewer's community service work which you also may share. Whatever you do, don't neglect the small talk. It may well become the most important conversation of the interview as you establish common ground that binds you much closer to the interviewer than the 100+ questions he or she has prepared for you to answer.

The interviewer may next talk about the purpose of the interview as he or she attempts to focus the interview session around both the company and the position. At this point the interviewer may be very persuasive, even attempting to "sell" you on the position. Most of the interview time will be spent on the "drawing out information" phase—which is the primary focus of the remainder of this chapter. The remaining phases of the interview relate to questions you will ask (Chapter 7) and the close (Chapter 8). A final type of questions, which actually constitute a separate type of interview, relate to salary negotiations. Questions of salary may be raised near the end of the first employment interview or may be left for a later interview. Salary negotiations are examined in two of our other books—***Interview For Success*** and ***Dynamite Salary Negotiations***.

Interviewer's Questioning Concerns and Techniques

Always keep in mind what interviewers are trying to achieve through the verbal interchange. They know hiring is a risky and expensive business. They never know what they are really getting until the individual starts performing in their organization.

The employer wants someone who can do the job well—someone worth the salary and benefits. The employer also wants someone who will be a good representative to others outside the organization. The person should be able to get along well with supervisors and co-workers inside the organization. Translating these concerns into questions, most interviewers want to know:

- Why should I hire you?
- What kind of person are you?
- What kind of employee will you make in our organiza-tion—willingness to take responsibility as well as direc-tions, be productive, loyal, creative, entrepreneurial, enthusiastic?
- Do you have a demonstrated and sustained interest in this work?
- Do your credentials demonstrate that you are a purposeful individual who gets things done?
- How much will you cost us?
- What haven't you told us about yourself?
- What are your weaknesses?

- Will you be able to work with your supervisors and other employees in this organization?
- How long will you stay with us before you start looking for another job?

While most interviewers will not bluntly ask you these questions, they will seek answers by asking other questions which may give them cues to your behavior.

Above all, they have invited you to the interview because they need information that goes beyond both your resume and a telephone screening interview. In this face-to-face conversational situation, interviewers will be looking for indicators of your

- expertise and competence
- motivation
- interpersonal skills
- decision-making skills
- interest in the job
- personality and likability

What you say will give the interviewer information in determining if you are the appropriate person for the position. Therefore, make sure all your answers are oriented toward these indicators. They must be formulated in such a way that they communicate both positive form and content.

While some interviewers may purposefully put you under a great deal of stress, most trained and experienced interviewers will conduct the interview in a professional manner. Most interviewers follow six rules when conducting interviews:

1. The interviewer will be sensitive to the candidate, respect his or her intelligence, and not act superior.

2. The interviewer will try to put the candidate at ease rather than create stress.

3. Following the initial "icebreakers," the interviewer will state the objective of the interview.

4. The interviewer will try to get the candidate to talk as much as possible without drilling him or her with questions.

5. The interviewer will seek valid information and not interject personal opinions into the interview. He or she will be professional at all times.

6. The interviewer will know when and how to close the interview. This includes clearly summarizing the candidate's interview statements so there will be no misunderstandings about what was communicated.

You can expect to encounter several types of questions which constitute different interviewing techniques:

- direct and indirect
- general and specific
- structured and unstructured
- open-ended and close-ended
- stressful
- hypothetical
- interpretive
- loaded
- multiple choice

While you can expect to encounter someone who has previous

interviewing experience and thus conducts the interview in a professional and competent manner, you may also encounter someone with little experience and who asks irrelevant, illegal, or stressful questions. In this case, you need to be tactful in how you respond to the interviewer's questions. You may need to take some initiative to keep the interview on track so you can best emphasize your strengths. If an interviewer's question seems too broad or vague, try to refocus the question by asking a clarifying question:

> By _____ do you mean _____?

This question should transform a vague question into something that is more manageable for you to answer. It should give better direction to your answer.

Interviewee's Ways of Answering Questions

Every time you answer a question, you should analyze your listener, use supports, and communicate positive form and content. The concepts of positive form and positive content stress the importance of avoiding negatives by always presenting yourself in as positive a light as possible. Analyzing your audience and using supports stresses the importance of using a language appropriate for the situation.

Use Positive Form

Several opportunities arise during the interview for you to enhance your image through the use of positive form. The first use of positive form relates to **names**. Each of us likes to be called by our name. Make sure you get the name of the interviewer, get it right, and use it from time to time as you speak. Use the interviewer's title (Miss, Mrs., Mr., Dr., Professor, etc.) and last name. Never call the interviewer by his or her first name unless specially requested to do so—even if the interviewer uses your first name. Many interviewers will be offended by such familiarity.

The second use of positive form is inherent in the **way you phrase questions and answers**. For example, rather than ask *"What are the duties of _____ position?"* ask *"What would be my duties?"* This form of questioning subtly plants the positive thought of you in the position. This is not presumptuous because you used the word *"would,"* which indicates you are not overly sure of yourself.

A third use of positive form relates to **good grammar**. Proper use of language is not something to be left in the English classroom. Many so-called "educated" people do not use good grammar, and many of these people do not interview successfully. Check your use of grammar. If it is not impeccable, make an effort to improve it before the interview.

Fourth, use **good diction**. One of the most common problems is to shorten words. How many people do you hear say *"goin"* instead of *"going,"* or *"gonna"* rather than *"going to"*? Another problem is substituting, eliminating, or adding on consonants *"Adlanta"* rather than *"Atlanta,"* *"din't"* rather than *"didn't,"* *"idear"* rather than *"idea."* Do you do this? Do you ever say *"yea"* rather than *"yes"*? The use of sloppy speech is a habit many people—including the well educated—get into. But it is a habit—learned and reinforced behavior—you can change. If you have a tendency to modify words in these manners, it is a habit worth correcting.

Fifth, avoid using **vocalized pauses**. An occasional silence is acceptable and preferable to overuse of *"ahs"* and *"uhms."* Try not to fill silences with *"ah"* or *"and ah."* Vocalized pauses distract the listener from your message and the excessive use can be annoying.

Sixth, avoid the use of **fillers**. Fillers add no information and, if overdone, also distract the listener. The most commonly used fillers are *"you know," "like,"* and *"okay."* If used frequently, the listener becomes distracted and will find it hard to concentrate on the content of your message. They may also assume you have a speech problem!

Seventh, use **active verbs**. When talking about what you have done or will do, active verbs like *"organized," "analyzed,"* or *"supervised"* are preferable to the nouns *"organizer," "analyst,"* or *"supervisor."* Avoid the passive voice. For example, instead of saying *"The entire conference was organized by me"* (passive), say *"I organized the entire conference"* (active).

Eighth, avoid using **tentative, indecisive terms**, such as *"I think," "I guess,"* or *"I feel."* If you use them excessively, they will negatively affect the impression you are trying to leave with the interviewer. Research indicates that women use these tentative terms more frequently than men. By using these indecisive terms, you can—male or female—appear indecisive and somewhat muddled. You want to communicate that you are a clear and purposeful individual.

Most people could improve their use of positive form. But it's difficult for someone to follow those suggestions after reading them the night before the interview. One needs to begin making the necessary changes well in advance of the interview. It can be done if one really wants to make the changes, but for most people it takes concerted effort over time.

Analyze Your Listener and Use Supports

Public speakers are always advised to analyze both their audience and their situation before speaking. The same advice should be followed when you interview. **The language you use should vary**

according to the interviewer. If the interviewer is from the personnel office with little or no background in your field of expertise, your language should be less technical than it would be if you were talking with someone who shares your technical background. If you are interviewing with someone in your area of expertise, who also has the technical background, you should use a vocabulary relevant to the job in order to build common ground as well as your credibility. But don't overdo the use of jargon.

Analysis of your situation should tell you this is not the time for excessive modesty. Of course, you do not want to become an obnoxious braggart, but you do want to present your strengths—skills and accomplishments—in a positive way. Therefore, don't be reluctant to **talk about yourself and your accomplishments**. Remember, the interviewer wants to know more about you, especially your potential value to him or her. The more positive information you can communicate to the interviewer, the stronger your position will be in the final hiring decision.

When you make statements about your skills or accomplishments, try to back them up with **supports**. Can you give an **example** of how you improved production on your last job? Can you **describe** the sales campaign that won you the Best Copywriter of the Year Award? Can you **compare** the previous bookkeeping system with the one you instituted that saved your last employer so much money? Can you cite figures that demonstrate how you increased sales at the last company you worked for?

When you back up your assertions with supports, you gain several advantages over individuals who do not. Supports help clarify your comments; help substantiate them; help the listener recall them at a later time; and they add interest. Supports include such things as:

- examples
- illustrations

- descriptions
- definitions
- statistics
- comparisons
- testimonials

Use such supports to emphasize your accomplishments. While you may have included a few of these supports in your resume, the interview is the time to expand upon your accomplishments by using many of these supports.

A frequent question asked by prospective interviewees is *"How honest should I be?"* Most individuals have something in their background they believe would work against them in getting the job if the interviewer knew about it. They wonder if they should tell the interviewer before he or she finds out. We advise you to be honest—but not stupid. In other words, if asked a direct question about the thing you hoped to hide, answer honestly, but emphasize positives. Under no circumstances should you volunteer your negatives or weaknesses. The next section will show you some ways to manage questions about your weaknesses.

Use Positive Content

The actual content of your answers should be stated in the positive. One example of this is the type of hobbies you communicate to employers. As John Molloy notes, many employers prefer "active" hobbies, such as swimming, tennis, golfing, or jogging, to more sedentary activities, such as reading and stamp collecting.

But the most important examples of positive content relate to managing the specific interview questions which are designed to probe your knowledge, abilities, motivations, strengths, and weaknesses. The employer's goal is somewhat negative in the interview; he or she wants to know why **not** to hire you. The major unstated question is "What are your weaknesses?" Several other questions may be asked to indirectly answer this major one.

You should always phrase your answers to questions in a positive manner. Avoid the use of such commonly used negatives as *"can't," "didn't,"* and *"wouldn't."* These terms direct listeners into negative avenues of thinking. They do not communicate optimism and enthusiasm—two qualities you should demonstrate in the interview. Take, for example, two different answers to the following interview question.

QUESTION: Why did you major in business administration?

ANSWER 1: *That's real funny. I wanted to major in history, but my parents told me if they were footing the bills, I shouldn't be studying useless subjects. I tried political science, biology, and accounting but didn't like any of them. Business administration wasn't that difficult for me. I couldn't think of anything I like more—except perhaps history. And it's not a bad field to be in these days.*

ANSWER 2: *I always enjoyed business and wanted to make it a career. As a youth I had my own paper route, sold books door to door, and was a member of Junior Achievement. In college I was involved in a couple of small businesses. It seems as though I have always been in business. I tend to have a knack for it, and I love it. My major in business administration further strengthened my desire to*

go into business. It gave me better direction.
What I want is to work with a small and
growing firm that would use my abilities to
plan and implement marketing strategies.

While the first answer may be the most truthful, it presents a negative and haphazard image of you. The second answer, while also truthful, stresses the positive by communicating strengths, purpose, and enthusiasm.

Let's take as another example an employer who asks the interviewee why he is leaving his present job:

QUESTION: Why do you want to leave your job?

ANSWER 1: *After working there three years, I don't feel*
I'm going anywhere. Morale isn't very good,
and the management doesn't reward us
according to our productivity. I really don't
like working there anymore.

ANSWER 2: *After working there three years, I have*
learned a great deal about managing people
and developing new markets. But it is time
for me to move on to a larger and more
progressive organization where I can use my
marketing experience in several different
areas. I am ready to take on more responsi-
bilities. This change will be a positive step
in my professional growth.

Again, the first answer communicates too many negatives. The second answer is positive and upbeat in its orientation toward skills, accomplishments, and the future.

Most interview questions can be answered by using positive language that further emphasizes that you are competent, intelligent, friendly, spontaneous, honest, and likable. This language should project your strengths, purpose, and enthusiasm. If you feel you need to practice formulating positive responses to interview questions, examine the sample questions outlined in the remainder of this chapter. Consider alternative positive responses to each question. You also may want your spouse or friend to ask you interview questions. Tape record the interview and review your responses. Are your answers positive in both form and content? Do they communicate your strengths, purpose, and enthusiasm? Keep practicing the interview until you automatically respond with positive yet truthful answers.

How to Overcome Objections and Negatives

Interviewers are likely to have certain objections to hiring you. Some of their objections may be legitimate whereas others are misunderstandings. Objections might relate to any of the illegal questions outlined at the end of this chapter—marital status, sex, or age. But many objections are perfectly legal and are common ways of differentiating one candidate from another. Among these objections are questions relating to your bona fide qualifications—education, experience, and skills.

If you are weak in any of the qualification areas, you may not be able to overcome the objections unless you acquire the necessary qualifications. But chances are these qualifications have been screened prior to the interview and thus will not be enough to automatically preclude you from consideration. If your education, experience, and skill level pose any objections to the interviewer, stress again your strengths in a positive and enthusiastic manner. Objections to your educational background will be the easiest to deal with if your experience and skills demonstrate your value.

On the other hand, one objection individuals increasingly encounter today from employers is being **over-qualified**. More and more people by choice are moving **down** in their careers rather than up. Given the desire for and ease of higher education, more and more people appear over-educated for many jobs today.

Employers' objections to candidates being over-qualified are a legitimate concern. From the perspective of employers, the over-qualified individual may quickly become a liability. Becoming unhappy with the job, they leave after a short period of time. Other individuals may have an unrealistic ambition of quickly moving up the organizational ladder. In either case, the over-qualified individual may cost an employer more than he or she is worth.

The over-qualified candidate may think he or she is doing the employer a favor—the company is getting more for their money. If this is your perception of your value, you need to change it immediately. Unless you are prepared to take a position which is beneath your qualifications and can clearly communicate your desire to the employer so as to lessen his or her fears, you will most likely not get the job. In the interview you must convince the employer that you understand his apprehension about you, but you are willing, able, and eager to do the job.

While you want to communicate your strengths, employers want to know your weaknesses. There are several ways to handle questions that try to get at your weaknesses. If the interviewer frankly asks you *"What are some of your weaknesses?"*, be prepared to give him or her positive responses. You can do this in any of four different ways:

1. Discuss a negative which is not related to the job being considered:

I don't enjoy accounting. I know it's important, but I find it boring. Even at home my wife takes care of our books.

Marketing is what I like to do. Other people are much better at bookkeeping than I am. I'm glad this job doesn't involve any accounting!

2. Discuss a negative which the interviewer already knows:

I spent a great deal of time working on advanced degrees, as indicated in my resume, and thus I lack extensive work experience. However, I believe my education has prepared me well for this job. My leadership experience in college taught me how to work with people, organize, and solve problems. I write well and quickly. My research experience helped me analyze, synthesize, and develop strategies.

3. Discuss a negative which you managed to improve upon:

I used to get over-committed and miss important deadlines. But then I read a book on time management and learned what I was doing wrong. Within three weeks I reorganized my use of time and found I could meet my deadlines with little difficulty. The quality of my work improved. Now I have time to work out at the gym each day. I'm doing more and feeling better at the same time.

4. Discuss a negative that can also be seen as a positive:

I'm somewhat of a workaholic. I love my work, but I sometimes neglect my family because of it. I've been

going into the office seven days a week, and I often put in
12 hour days. I'm now learning to better manage my time
and my life.

Take Initiative

Employment recruiters on college campuses indicate that the most appealing candidates are those who take some initiative during the interview. You need to provide complete answers, using many of the supports we discussed earlier as you communicate your positive qualities to employers. You need to demonstrate depth of knowledge and abilities by going beyond short and superficial answers. You need to ask questions as well as respond to those asked of you. At least 50 percent of the conversation should be carried by you. If the interviewer is doing 70 to 80 percent of the talking, you will sense the interview is probably not going well!

We are not suggesting that you take control of the interview, but you need not play a completely passive role either. Taking initiative is a quality many employers prize in their employees. Indeed, many employers wish they could find more employees who would take initiative.

Even with the best interviewer, you will need to ask questions. Remember, you have a decision to make too. Are you really interested in the job? Does it fit your goals and skills? Will it give you the chance to do something you do well and enjoy doing? Will it give you an opportunity to move in some of the directions you want to move? Use the interview situation to get answers to these and other questions that are critical to your future. In Chapter 7 we address this issue of you asking questions of the interviewer. Throughout this chapter and the remainder of the book we identify 101 of the most important questions and answers to interview questions.

Questions and Answers

Expect to be asked numerous questions about your background, personality, experience, knowledge, skills, abilities, accomplishments, and goals. While the exact combination of questions will vary with the interviewer, you can expect several of the following questions to arise in most interviews.

Personal

Personal questions are often sensitive questions given today's litigious employment environment. This area of questioning sometimes includes illegal questions.

In many cases, the interviewer will ask indirect questions to probe your personal situation, such as age, marital status, family situation, income stability, or class. For example, instead of asking about your age, he may ask when you graduated from high school or college and then do some quick arithmetic to calculate your age within one or two years of accuracy.

Instead of asking if you are married, divorced, or single, he may ask if your spouse has had a chance to visit the community. If he wants to know if you have children and a stable family situation, he may ask if your family is interested in information on private schools.

Religion can be handled by making reference to holidays: **"Do you have any special religious holidays you need to observe?"**

If he wants to know if you financially stable, he might ask you **"Do you feel your current salary is sufficient given your lifestyle?"**

The question of class may be handled by asking where you currently live or plan to live in the community as well as if you rent or own a home; home ownership and neighborhood locational patterns are good indicators of income and status levels as well as community stability.

Be prepared to answer these questions with tact. If the question is direct and illegal, try to manage it as best possible (see section on illegal questions). If the question is indirect, also be tactful, knowing full well you are being asked a personal question which could have negative consequences for you. If, for example, you are asked **"Do you rent or own a home?"**, do more than just indicate one or the other. If you say you rent, the interviewer may interpret this as a sign of potential community and financial instability. You might answer by turning this potential negative indicator into a positive:

I've been renting a townhouse during the past three years. That worked well for the first two years. But I've now outgrown it. And I know I'm losing money by not building equity in a home. I plan to either purchase or build a home within the next two years.

This answer indicates you are in transition. You view homeownership as a wise financial investment. Money doesn't appear to be a problem—only timing and the right location.

Questions about other personal subjects should be handled in a similar manner. Turn what appears to be a potential negative question into a positive outcome.

Education

If you are a recent graduate with very little long-term work experience, your education will most likely be your major qualification in the eyes of most employers. Interviewers will look at education as an indicator of your potential to learn and grow in their organization. If they refer to your resume, the only information they may have is the educational institutions you attended, graduation dates, majors, and any special recognitions or extracurricular activities, such as a high G.P.A., scholarships, or offices held. They may ask numerous questions relating to your education-related experiences. Expect to encounter several of these questions:

- **Why did you attend _____ university?**
- **Why did you major in _____?**
- **What was your minor?**
- **What subjects did you enjoy the most?**
- **What subjects did you enjoy the least?**

These questions attempt to probe your **motivation** for making certain educational choices. When you answer these questions, make sure you demonstrate that you made conscious and rational choices, even though your choices may have been haphazard and accidental at the time. For example, when asked why you attended a particular university, formulate your answer in a positive manner:

I decided on Bowers College because of its strong liberal arts tradition and its international program. The college has an excellent reputation for individualized learning and operates a fine semester abroad program which I participated in during the Fall of 1993. It also gave me an opportunity to participate in excellent band and student government programs. After visiting more than 15 different colleges, I decided Bowers College was the best place for me given my particular interests and career goals. In the end, it was the right decision. I really enjoyed my four years there, including a wonderful semester abroad in France. I

*learned a great deal and made some terrific friendships with
both faculty and students.*

This answer stresses that fact that you made a conscious choice
after considering your options. You had specific goals which were
met by attending this institution. In other words, you demonstrate
strong motivation, clear thinking, and a sense of purpose. More-
over, your experience confirmed you made the right choice.

The same principle holds true when asked **"Why did you
major in _____?"**

*I chose history because I always enjoyed the rigorous
tradition of analyzing events, formulating theories, conducting research, and writing reports. While many people may
think this is not a useful major, I believe it has prepared me
well for the type of work I want to do. History really helped
me develop some excellent research and writing skills,
especially in using computers. I can quickly analyze most
issues or problems and reformulate them into agenda items
for directing brainstorming and group problem-solving
sessions.*

Other questions you may be asked about your education relate
to your achievements, grades, and your future. You might be asked

**If you had to do it all over again, what would you have
changed about your college education?**

This question tests your judgment concerning everything from
choosing an institution to selecting a major, taking courses, and
participating in educational life. It may also probe what you feel
you have learned from the college experience. There are many
ways to respond to this question—both positive and negative. We

suggest that you again focus on the positive. If, for example, your grades were not exceptional and you know the interviewer knows this, you might want to take a potential negative and turn it into a positive:

> *If I had to do it over again, I would have spent more time developing good study skills during my first two years. Like many other freshmen and sophomores, I quickly got involved in extracurricular activities. I joined everything and my grades suffered accordingly. I really got down to business during my junior year and my grades improved considerably. I just wish I had done that earlier.*

This answer demonstrates that you recognize your grades were a negative. It also demonstrates that you learned and improved yourself.

On the other hand, the interviewer may ask you a direct question about your grades if he knows they were not great:

You obviously were not a star performer in college. Why didn't you do better than a G.P.A. of 2.6?

This is not the time to confess your weaknesses, although your G.P.A. indicates you are at best "average." If you say *"I really don't know,"* you indicate you are indeed average. Again, be prepared to answer this in the positive. You might use the same strategy as in the previous question—your first two years were not good, but you learned and improved considerably during your last two years. Alternatively, the following may apply to you:

> *College was not easy for me. I was the first person in my family to attend college. While I did have a small scholarship to help with tuition expenses, I worked all four years*

earning 80 percent of my educational expenses while carrying full course loads each semester. I wish I had had more time to devote to my studies but I was working 30 hour weeks at part-time jobs. I know I could have done better, especially during my first two years and in nonmajor courses. However, I did receive a 3.5 G.P.A. in my major.

Employers will also want to know something about your college experiences outside the classroom. These may tell them something about your personality, leadership abilities, and level of energy. You might encounter some of these questions:

- **What types of extracurricular activities did you participate in during college?**

- **I noticed you worked on the student newspaper. Can you tell me about your work? What did you do?**

- **Did you join many groups while attending college? Which ones did you enjoy the most? The least? What was your role?**

- **What leadership positions did you hold in college?**

- **Did you work while also attending college? Full-time? Part-time?**

Keep your answers focused on relating specific experiences to the interviewer's interests—how you will best fit into his job. Many of these extracurricular activities should emphasize your leadership abilities, participative behavior, and entrepreneurial skills. For the employer, they may be good predictors of future on-the-job performance. You'll be demonstrating that you learned and accomplished more in college than just subject matter and grades. You have energy beyond the stereotypical sedentary student who always "hit the books."

Finally, the interviewer may want to hear from you what you think is the relationship between your educational experience and the job for which you are interviewing:

How does your degree prepare you for working as a _____?

Answer this question by stressing how your knowledge, skills, and abilities acquired in college have a direct or indirect bearing on the job. Don't focus on the subjects or courses you took; these are of less interest to employers than what you can do for them in terms of using specific job-related skills that may have been acquired while in school. Employers especially look for individuals with strong communication, analytic, and problem-solving abilities and who are flexible, trainable, and enthusiastic. Above all, they like people who demonstrate **energy and drive**. Therefore, try to think of your college experience in terms of these key skills and qualities. Do you, for example, communicate better—both orally and in writing—because of your college experience? Do you demonstrate problem-solving or leadership abilities because of your extracurricular activities in student government, on a sports team, or as a member of a fraternity or sorority? Are you an enthusiastic individual who approaches new tasks with energy and drive? Are you open-minded and willing to learn new things? Do you get along well with others, especially those in superior positions? You answer these questions by stressing those skills that are most likely to **transfer** to the job.

If some time has passed since you graduated and you have several years of subsequent work experience, the interviewer may ask few questions about your educational background. He will most likely focus on your work experience, or how your education prepared you for the work you do. Expect to be asked:

- **Why did you choose to attend _____ university?**

- **How did your major relate to your work after graduation?**

- **I notice you have an MBA. What do you think about working with people who have MBAs? Are they really as sharp as we are led to believe?**

- **I see you majored in history but you've been selling pharmaceuticals during the past 15 years. Do you feel it was a mistake majoring in history?**

- **If you had to do it all over again, what would you major in and what degrees would you pursue?**

- **Are you planning to take any additional graduate work during the next few years?**

- **Have you ever thought of changing careers by going back to school to get another degree? What would you like to do if you had a chance to take two years off and return to the university as a full-time student?**

If you graduated several years ago, the interviewer may want to know about your educational and training progress in recent years. He may be looking for indicators of your willingness to keep current in your field as well as learn new skills. You might, for example, encounter some of these questions about your education and training experiences:

- Have you regularly participated in company-sponsored education and training programs? Could you elaborate on which ones you attended, for how long, and what you felt you learned in the process?

- If you had a choice of three one-week training programs to attend, which ones do you feel you would benefit the most from? Why?

- You said you didn't know how to use a computer. Everyone here does use the computer, even top executives. Is this something you plan to learn soon?

- How much time do you spend each month keeping up with new developments in your field?

- Which trade and professional journals do you regularly read and subscribe to?

- How many professional conferences or seminars do you attend each year? Which ones are you planning to attend this year?

- What are your educational goals for the next 5 years?

You should answer each of these questions in as positive a manner as possible. Employers want to hire individuals who are continuously learning and adapting to changes in their field.

Other questions concerning your education might include:

- How did you finance your education?

- Why didn't you decide to go to college?

- Why didn't you go on for a graduate degree?

- Why did you drop out of college after your second year?

- Why did you decide to join the military before going to college?

- What didn't you like about school?

- What did you normally do during your summer breaks?

- Who was your favorite teacher? What did she do differently from the others?

- Why didn't you participate in more extracurricular activities?

- Do you think your grades reflect how well you will do on this job?

Questions may relate to learning beyond formal education. The rapidly changing face of business today forces the successful job seeker to continually upgrade her skills. The interviewer is interested both in *whether* you continue to upgrade your skills as well as in *what* skills you are learning or improving.

- What is the most recent skill you have learned?

  If you have learned or upgraded several skills recently, select the one you believe enhances a performance area required for the job you hope to land as a result of this interview. For example,

Although I have given a lot of presentations in my present job, I did not feel as comfortable giving speeches as I wanted to. So two months ago I took a 3-day seminar in public speaking. I had a great instructor who not only helped me polish my preparation and presentation skills, but helped me feel more comfortable giving speeches as well. I took her advice to seek out additional opportunities to gain experience and self-confidence by joining a local Toastmasters group. I have given 5 speeches over the past six weeks and now I look forward to each opportunity to give a talk.

This response demonstrates the interviewee took the initiative to improve a skill, learned from the classroom experience, and went beyond it by seeking additional opportunities to practice his skills.

Experience

Questions relating to your experience will attempt to clarify how qualified you are for the job beyond what appears in your resume. Some questions may be technical in nature—testing your ability to work with special equipment, programs, people, routines—whereas other questions relate to your overall experience. Expect to encounter several of these questions:

■ **What are your qualifications?**

Here you want to stress your skills and accomplishments in reference to the position in question. Give examples and use numbers whenever possible. For example,

I have over 10 years of progressively responsible experience with pharmaceutical sales. Each year I have exceeded my performance goals by at least 15 percent and expanded my client base by 10 percent. My previous employers consistently praised me as one of their top five salespeople. I will bring to this job a proven record of performance as well as several key accounts worth more than $1.2 million in annual sales.

If education is an important qualifying criteria, be sure to include reference to your educational background, degrees, and accomplishments.

- **What experience do you have for this job?**

Again, as in the previous question, stress your skills and accomplishments rather than formal job duties and responsibilities assigned to your position.

- **What do you like most about your present job/most recent job?**

This question is designed to get at your work values. Try to stress the same values held by the employer—focus on performance and getting the job done. Avoid any reference to self-centered values, such as salary and benefits. For example,

I really enjoy working with a team of competent, energetic, and innovative professionals in developing and implementing projects. During the past three years I've had a chance to work closely with two of the industry's best project managers. I

learned a great deal about how to make decisions and implement them in a timely manner. I'm looking forward to working in a similar environment that encourages team efforts, initiative, and risk-taking. But most important of all, I enjoy seeing the results of such efforts translated into satisfied customers and new projects.

- **What do you like least about your present job/most recent job?**

The reverse of the previous question, answer this one in a similar manner, keeping in mind the principles for handling possible negatives. It's best to mention a negative you managed to improve upon because such an example stresses your initiative and problem solving abilities. For example,

I didn't like always having to crisis manage and work overtime to meet deadlines. I like to see my work get done on time and with the least amount of stress. During the first year with XYZ Company I was usually in a reactive mode—always in a crisis trying to meet project deadlines. I got the work done but I never had time to do the thoughtful planning and scheduling that was necessary to meet those deadlines. I had inherited that system from my predecessor. But during the second year I developed a new planning and scheduling system that enabled our division to meet all of our deadlines with minimal crisis management. This gave us more time to realistically plan projects and meet all requirements within the designated time frames. It also saved the *company more than $30,000 in overtime salaries. Morale increased tremendously, and I believe we became a much more productive workforce because of this planning and scheduling system.*

- **What do you like most about your present or most recent boss?**

Focus on something that demonstrates your appreciation for sound supervisory principles rather than focus on the personality or personal characteristics of the individual. You want to generalize beyond this specific case as you link your observations to the position for which you are interviewing. For example,

My current boss is a terrific role model who really knows how to work well with her employees. She doesn't expect her subordinates to do things she wouldn't do. In fact, she has an open-door policy where everyone has easy access to her and where open two-way communication is encouraged. She has created a very congenial and supportive work environment where everyone performs to their best level. What I really like about her is her constant and sincere effort to assist her subordinates. She regularly asks us "How are you doing? Can I be of any help? Let me know if you have any questions." She's genuinely concerned that we do the very best we can. She knows the strengths of each employee and tries to use them in the best possible combination. Her subordinates really admire her. They go that "extra mile" to produce quality work. Someday I would like to become such a supervisor.

- **What do you like least about your present/most recent boss?**

Be careful with this question. What negative things you say about your past bosses probably reflect what negative things you will say about your future bosses. Even though you may have had conflicts with a previous boss, focus on a negative that can also be interpreted as a positive. For example,

> *What I least liked was the lack of feedback on my performance. My boss of five years ago always gave his subordinates immediate feedback on their performance—whether positive or negative. You always knew where you stood with him. I got used to working in such an environment where open communication between supervisors and subordinates was actively encouraged. I assumed that was how supervision normally operated. But when I moved to XYZ Corporation, the management style and organizational culture were very different. The company relied heavily on its annual performance evaluation to communicate with its employees. And my supervisor always gave me outstanding annual performance evaluations. Furthermore, he was an extremely competent individual who I really enjoyed working with and learned a great deal from. But he just didn't give his subordinates much feedback on a day-to-day basis. I later learned that may have been just his style. But I've learned to operate well under two different styles of supervision and two different organizational cultures. I think his weakness actually benefitted me in the long-run.*

■ **How does your present job (or most recent) relate to the overall goals of your department/the company?**

Again, you want to answer this question in very clear, performance terms. Before going to the interview, think how your job fits into the larger organizational scheme. What is it you do that promotes the goals of the organization? Better still, try to demonstrate how you might have taken initiative to **expand** your job into an even more important job than originally envisioned by the company. Such an observation demonstrates taking important **initiative** on your part. An applicant might, for example, answer the question in this manner:

> *When I first began, the job required that I do routine editing using the old paper and pencil technique and often burning the midnight oil. I would be assigned an article or report and sit down for several hours looking for organizational, grammatical, and spelling errors. Since I'm patient, a detail person, and somewhat tenacious, I enjoyed the work, but it wasn't particularly exciting. Anyone with a basic background in editing could do this job. However, during my second year, I took advantage of a special computer editing course sponsored by the local community college. The course opened a whole new world of editing for me. I learned how to use several state-of-the-art computer editing programs. I then persuaded my supervisor to request management to invest in one of the programs. Since I already had the skills, they agreed to let me bring the program on-line for a six month experimental period. Well, within one month I was able to produce dramatic*

results for my supervisor and management—we reduced editing time by 60 percent and errors by 20 percent. Management immediately invested in several other editing programs which saved the company nearly $40,000 in freelance editing fees during the first year. I'm now in charge of managing our new computerized programs, which involves training employees, customizing programs, and updating software. Even with my new responsibilities, I still do a lot of editing. The job is now more fun, and I feel much more productive. It's now an exciting job that is very important to the overall operation of the company.

Accomplishments and Work Style

- **What is your greatest strength?**

This question should be answered with a skill and accomplishment that is directly related to the employer's needs. Avoid strengths that tend to emphasize your personal characteristics, such as your values or attitudes. Instead, focus on those things you both do well and enjoy doing related to your experience and qualifications. We especially like strengths that indicate your capacity to adapt and learn in new work settings. For example,

I've always adapted well to new work situations with a great deal of energy, drive, and initiative. I like taking on new challenges and working with people who have clear goals in mind. But I'm not just a "starter" who gets bored after the "new" becomes "routine." I like getting things started and seeing them to the very end. I guess I would say my greatest strength is keeping focused on what needs to be done, and then doing it.

- **What is your greatest weakness?**

Be careful with this question. This is not the time to confess a weakness that can be interpreted as a negative and thus disqualify you from further consideration. Using the principle of turning a negative into a positive, select a weakness that can also be interpreted as a strength, as we discussed earlier in this chapter. Our favorite example of confessing a weakness is the workaholic syndrome—a weakness that has been improved upon:

My major weakness is that I'm somewhat of a workaholic. I love my work, but I sometimes neglect my family because of it. I often go into the office seven days a week and frequently put in 12-hour days. I'm now learning to better manage my time— and my family. And I believe I'm also more energetic and productive because of these changes.

This response also follows the principle of "being honest, but not stupid." We are sure you can come up with examples that fit your situation and follow this principle on handling questions about your weaknesses. Whatever you do, don't be coy by saying *"Oh, I don't have any weaknesses."* That would also be stupid. Everyone has weaknesses, but you need not confess things that might knock you out of further consideration for the job.

■ **What are the two things you would like to improve about yourself?**

Again, beware of this question which is an indirect way of asking about your weaknesses. You can easily slip up and confess your weaknesses by merely identifying what needs to be improved. Keep focused on the employer's needs—not your greed. For example,

> *The two things I would really like to improve on over the next two years are my supervisory experience and computer skills. I already know supervision and computers well, but I would like to do even better. I'm going to take some special courses to help me improve in these areas.*

■ **What are some of the reasons for your success?**

This is not the time to become an obnoxious bore. Focus on a particular attitude **and** skill that may contribute to your success. These might be generic attitudes and skills the interviewer already knows are ingredients to success. Your response should be thoughtful and engaging, confirming that you have the necessary ingredients in place to become successful in this company. One might answer the question in this manner:

> *I attribute much of my success to one of my college mentors who instilled in me a particular attitude or philosophy about work and life in general. He stressed the importance of being both competent and tenacious. I've always tried to improve my skills either on the job or through special training pro-*

grams. I approach my work with enthusiasm and stick with it until it's done, however difficult and challenging it may be. I don't have time to find excuses for not doing something or pushing work off on to others. I think this particular stick-to-it attitude has served me well. And I try to instill a similar attitude in others I work with. I think success comes to those who know what they want to do, where they are going, and put in the necessary effort to see that things get accomplished.

- **Tell me about an on-going responsibility in your current/most recent job that you enjoyed.**

Focus on a responsibility that you believe is essential to the job you are interviewing for as well as important to your current or most recent position.

- **What duties in your present/most recent job do you find it difficult to do?**

Try to identify things that either are not part of the job description of the job you are interviewing for or that are a minor or unimportant part of the job.

With so many orders being shipped I sometimes find it difficult to keep up with filing of the shipping confirmations.

- **Describe your typical work day.**

This question is aimed at getting some sense of how you orient yourself to the workplace. What exactly do you do each day, from the time you arrive at the office to when you leave? Avoid giving a dull hour-by-hour chronology of your workday. Focus, instead, on stressing your enthusiasm for work, your key skills, and your daily accomplishments. For example,

> *My typical day involves a great deal of accounting work and meetings with the chief financial officer and bookkeeper. I usually begin by balancing the ledger and reporting yesterday's balance to the chief financial officer. I then meet with the bookkeeper to make sure all invoices have been posted and payments have been issued. The remainder of my day involves meetings with other financial officers to resolve any problems arising in the daily accounting process. I would say I'm mainly involved in managing our financial team and doing a great deal of trouble-shooting throughout the day.*

- **Do you anticipate problems or do you react to them?**

Obviously employers want to hire people who have a view of the big picture. They want individuals who can anticipate potential problems and hence avoid them or, at the very least, minimize the negative impact on the organization. At the same time, even the most adroit employee will occasionally find a problem is upon him and his only choice is to react. Cite examples of your past successes at anticipating potential problems before they can negatively impact the company or indicate the systems you put in place to assure that you get periodic information from subordinates so there will be few surprises.

- **How much business will you bring to our firm during the next year?**

This question is especially appropriate for individuals who work with a client base and who are expected to bring many of their clients with them to the new employer. For many lawyers, this is the most important question they may be asked in the interview. Law firms are less concerned with the work skills—research and consultation—of candidates than with their ability to bring with them paying clients who are the single most important resource for the company. A similar situation relates to other occupations, such as advertising and public relations, where a client base is key to the organization's operation. The answer to this question is very factual—tell the interviewer exactly how many clients you expect to bring as well as their total annual dollar value. Also, try to project how many additional clients you are likely to attract in the coming months.

- **Do you ever lose your temper?**

This question is aimed at uncovering one of your possible weaknesses. Again, be careful with your answer, even though you may occasionally lose your temper. For example,

> *I sometimes get irritated but I generally don't lose my temper. I've learned to separate my temper from my job.*

- **How do you deal with stressful situations?**

Here you should communicate what it is you do to manage stress. This is not the place to indicate you don't have stress because the job may very well come with a great deal of built-in stress. For example,

Over the years, I've learned to put stressful situations in better perspective than I used to. I know some stress comes with the job. If the stress involves the work of my subordinates, I usually open up lines of communication to deal with any issues contributing to the stress. If the stress is a result of the daily workload, I get through the day knowing full well my exercise routine at the end of the day will renew me both physically and mentally. I've also given up coffee which seems to contribute to stress and I've joined a health club.

- **What has your present/most recent supervisor criticized about your work?**

This is not the time to confess everything every supervisor has criticized you for. Two strategies are to either select a relatively unimportant element of your work that was criticized (or one unrelated to the job you are interviewing for) or turn the criticism into a positive by demonstrating how well you accepted the criticism and that you have corrected or are working to correct the problem. (See examples on pages 93-95)

- **How do you feel about working overtime and on weekends?**

Again, be honest but not stupid with this question. Avoid

using negative terms such as *"don't," "won't,"* or *"can't."* You might also turn this question around with a question of your own that subtly puts you into the position. For example,

> *I would expect to occasionally put in extra time since I know there are deadlines that sometimes must be met outside regular working hours. In general, how often should I expect to work overtime and on weekends in this position?*

- **How well do you work under deadlines?**

This question is designed to identify your work style. Do you stay around until the work gets done? Are you willing to put in overtime? Does the stress of deadlines get to you? Are you a peak performer given impending deadlines? The interviewer wants to know what type of performer you will be when deadlines come around. The most positive thing you could say is this:

> *While others may have difficulty managing deadlines, including experiencing a great deal of stress, I do well under stress. I tend to take charge, organize tasks, and move everything along quickly to get the job done. More importantly, I try to avoid doing things only at deadline time. My goal is to get tasks done well in advance so that we have more time to do the necessary evaluation required for producing a high quality product.*

- **How do you feel about the contributions you made to XYZ corporation?**

Be positive and specific since you are being asked to evaluate your performance with your present or former employer. Try to make a logical connection between your achievements with XYZ corporation and the needs of this employer. Use examples and numbers to emphasize your performance points. For example,

I really feel good about what I accomplished there. When I arrived, the division was in disarray. Morale was low, employee turnover was high, and performance was at best questionable. Within five months I managed to turn this situation around by implementing a new management system that gave employees greater say in what they were doing. Morale increased dramatically, employee turnover declined by 30 percent, and our division became one of the best performers in the organization. In fact, we also became the model for management changes that eventually took place in all other divisions. I think the organization as a whole performs much better today than ever before.

- **What do you wish you had accomplished in your present/most recent job but were unable to?**

Select examples of things you were on the way to accomplishing and could likely have accomplished with more time.

My goal was to cut customer complaints by 50%. In the past three months we've cut complaints by 40%. I think given another month we could reach the 50% mark.

- **What will you bring to this position that another candidate won't?**

Again, emphasize your skills, abilities, accomplishments, and experiences that may be unique in comparison to other candidates. An example that can be remembered may serve you well even though it may not illustrate a unique contribution. For example,

> *If I look carefully at my previous experience, I know there is one thing that really stands out: I'm successful at what I do. Take, for example, the time my supervisor asked me to develop a new approach to marketing typewriters. We knew we had a poor market situation since computers were quickly displacing typewriters. So I came up with the idea of marketing our Tatus Typewriter along with the Tatus Computer as part of a special Spring College Special. We learned many buyers were still reluctant to purchase a computer but they weren't sure if they should buy a typewriter. So we included a free typewriter with the computer. Our market research showed it was mainly the parents who made the purchase as a gift for their child. Many of these buyers could identify with the typewriter but not the computer. As a result of this marketing scheme, we realized a 330 percent increase in sales of both the typewriter and computer. It's this type of talent I will bring to your organization. I enjoy developing solutions to challenging problems. My supervisors usually turn to me for innovative marketing ideas that will work.*

- **How do you get along with your superiors?**

Whatever you say, make sure you communicate positive relations with your supervisors. The interviewer may be trying to get some indication of your attitudes toward superiors rather than an accounting of your behavior.

I generally work well with everyone. I especially work well with supervisors who regularly provide feedback on my performance. I had excellent relationships with my last two supervisors who rated me in the top five percent of the workforce in terms of cooperation and performance.

- **How do you get along with your co-workers?**

Employers want individuals who can work well together, who don't create interpersonal problems that get bounced up to supervisors, and who are productive as a team. You should indicate that you are a team player who works well in such an environment. For example,

I see myself as a team player. I enjoy the collegial atmosphere that often comes in working with fellow professionals. I also work especially well in one-on-one settings. I usual end up being the spokesman for the group and often emerge in leadership roles. My co-workers respect my work and often turn to me for advice.

- **How do you manage your subordinates?**

If you are interviewing for a supervisory position, make

sure you understand the principles of good supervision and use the language of supervision. This question is as much a test of your knowledge as a probe into your behavior vis-a-vis your subordinates.

- **How do you feel about working with superiors who may be less well educated, intelligent, or competent than you?**

This question may arise in some organizations where there is a distinct difference in educational, knowledge, and performance levels between the "old" versus "new" blood. Older organizations that have undergone recent rapid expansion often face this issue. You need to indicate that you are prepared to work in this situation, if indeed you are. At the same time, this is a good opportunity to get some "inside" information on the organization's potential management problems. For example,

> *I normally get along well with everyone in the organization regardless of their age, education, or experience. But quite frankly, I do have difficulty accepting poor performance, especially when it affects my work. If this is a problem here, I assume it is a management problem which will be dealt with at the management level. I expect to be evaluated according to my performance and that my performance would not be judged on the inabilities of others. Could you elaborate more on the nature of the problem?*

- **Do you prefer working with others or alone?**

Most organizations look for team players rather than loners. It's best to indicate you are a team player. Better still, indicate you do well in both types of situations. For example,

I'm a team player in most situations, although I normally don't seek the limelight. I'm quite content doing what I'm supposed to do. At the same time, I also work well alone on tasks that require individual initiative and creativity. I don't need a great deal of direction. Just let me know what needs to be done and I usually will find a way either alone or in consultation with others.

■ How do others view your work?

This question can be answered in many different ways. Keep in mind the so-called "others" can be supervisors, co-workers, subordinates, customers, or clients. Try to present evidence that your work is well respected by others for its quantity and quality. For example,

I'm generally viewed by those I work with as a dependable producer. My supervisors and co-workers often turn to me for advice and leadership. I also work well with clients, many of whom have been with me for more than five years.

■ How do you normally deal with criticism?

Here's another question designed to learn how you relate to others in the workplace. Acknowledge the reality of criticism, treat it as a positive force, and show how you have dealt with it. For example,

> _I value constructive criticism because it helps me do a better job. I'm a good listener who takes criticism seriously. If it's justified, I try to make the necessary changes. When it's unjustified, I probe the nature of the problem with questions. I've never really had a problem with criticism since I try to maintain open communication on the job. This enables me to deal with many problems before they become subjects for criticism._

- **Do you consider yourself a risk taker? Could you give me examples of risks you've taken in previous jobs?**

Be careful with this question. It can be a double-edge sword, especially if the organization does not want risk takers! Analyze the situation and assess whether risk taking is likely to be viewed as a positive in this organization. If you believe it is a plus, try to cite specific examples of what you've done. If you are unsure, you can answer this question by noting you do have some qualities of the risk taker, but you are also a very rational and responsible individual who is not reckless.

- **Do you consider yourself to be someone who takes greater initiative than others?**

Employers prize employees who take initiative since it means less time needs to be spent on many supervisory tasks. Assuming you do take initiative, indicate that you are someone who can be expected to take initiative on the job, perhaps more so than others. For example,

Yes, I do. Most of my jobs have afforded me a great deal of decision-making latitude, especially at the production level. In fact, initiative was literally institutionalized in my last job. I've worked with quality circles where we were expected to take initiative at all times, both as a team and as individuals. Could you tell me how initiative is handled here? How is decision-making structured in this organization? Would you say it's highly decentralized? Is initiative actively encouraged among employees in dealing with production issues?

- **Are you a self-starter? Could you give examples?**

Yes, I am able to take on a new assignment and run it successfully without supervision. When I was hired by Foremost Printers, they had just taken over a publication they did not want and did not know what to do with. They were in the business of printing and know nothing about publishing. They gave me the responsibility of running the publication. I didn't knew anything about publishing either, but I understood marketing, so I read and talked to people and learned what I needed to know. At the end of the first year the publication was running in the black, and by the end of the second year we had increased our subscriber base by over 300%.

- **Are you a good time manager?**

Time is one of the most precious commodities you have, and once squandered it can never be re-gained. Interviewers seek employees who can set goals and prioritize tasks to accomplish goals. For example,

> *I consistently meet deadlines. When circumstances beyond my control interfere, I re-prioritize my tasks as well as those of my staff so we can get right back on track.*

Then cite examples from your experience to support your claim that you are a good time manager.

Motivation

- **What is the most important thing you've learned from the jobs you've held?**

Try to combine task/skill elements with interpersonal elements. Or if you are interviewing for a job utilizing different skills than those used on your present and recent jobs, stress the people skills you've learned—whether it's to manage in a style that gets things done while maintaining good esprit d'corp or learning to follow directions and work cooperatively with co-workers.

- **Why should we hire you?**

This is often considered to be the knee-bender—it brings you to your knees before the employer who wants to know your real motivations for seeking employment with him. However, this should be one of the easiest questions to answer given the principles we previously discussed. You should stress how your skills and abilities relate to the employer's needs. It's time to toot your horn. Be as specific as possible. For example,

I assume you are looking for someone with a solid track record in sales and marketing of automotive parts. I will bring to this job 12 years of progressive experience in all phases of sales and marketing of both domestic and foreign automotive parts. In my last job I increased sales by 20 percent each year for the past five years. I have a consistent pattern of performance employers readily seek, including your competition. I would think this is something your organization would want to bring on board.

- **What really motivates you to perform?**

Focus again on job-related performance criteria rather than on other motivational criteria. For example,

What really motivates me is the nature of the work itself. I really enjoy my work, especially when I see the results in terms of actual increases in sales. I tend to focus on outcomes rather than duties or responsibilities.

- **Why do you want to work for _____?**

This question is much like the one on why they should hire you. Focus again on what you will bring to the job in reference to the employer's needs. You might also stress the importance of the organization to your career goals.

I've greatly admired your organization. Since I've worked for your competition during the past seven years, I've had a chance to regularly evaluate your work and at times out-perform your marketing team.

You provide an excellent service which I consider to be the best in the field. I also believe my experience and skills are such that I will make an excellent addition to your marketing team. I know your competition well and this knowledge, combined with my skills, should further strengthen your marketing efforts in the coming months when two new competitors will be entering your southern territory.

- **Why do you want to leave your present job? Why did you leave your previous jobs?**

Give positive rather than negative reasons for leaving, regardless of how negative your situation may have been. If you left because you were asked to resign or were unhappy, don't confess this negative. Instead, call it *"furthered career advancement"* or *"seeking a new challenge."* Avoid using negative terms. For example,

I left my last job after four years of progressive experience. As a small firm, it offered few opportunities for career advancement. I felt I had gone as far as I could there and decided it was time to expand my career horizons.

- **Why have you changed jobs so frequently?**
- **Why would you be more likely to stay here?**

Even though tenure with companies tends to be a lot shorter these days than a decade or two ago, employers are reluctant to hire people who have job-hopped excessively—especially if there seems to be no good reason for the frequent changes. Hiring and training employees is an investment the employer makes. She wants to get a reasonable return on that cost. Stress reasons why the situation(s) that caused you to job-hop no longer exist or what is different about this opportunity that will cause you to stay. Stress you intend this to be a longer-term commitment. For example,

> *I realize I did not stay long in the first three jobs I held after college. In each instance I had accepted positions in very small firms. I learned and rapidly gained proficiency each time, but found there was no place to advance. I was stuck in a dead-end job. With this job search I have limited my interest to firms like yours that are large enough for me to grow with the firm as my skills increase.*

- **Why do you want a job you are over-qualified for?**

If you apply for a job that appears to be beneath your qualifications, you may be asked why you want to step down the career ladder to such a job. In fact, many employers will object to hiring someone who appears over-qualified. You will need to come up with a bonafide explanation for your behavior. After all, you might leave within a very short period of time, thus creating another personnel problem for the employer. For example,

> *I know I may appear over-qualified for this position. Some employers may not want to hire me because they are afraid I will be unhappy and leave soon. However, I've given this a lot of thought. I'm really interested in this position, and I believe I could bring something to this job that others may not be*

able to. I prefer the location and the ability to develop a flexible work schedule. I'm committed to staying with the job for at least two years. During that time I think the position will grow in reference to my particular interests and skills. I believe you will be pleased working with me.

- **Are you willing to take a cut in pay from your present/most recent job? Why?**

Be careful with this question. It begins intruding into the salary negotiation phase of the interview. You are not ready to discuss money at this point, even though the interviewer may raise this question. Your goal is to learn about the worth of the position as well as communicate your value to the employer. If the interviewer raises this question, he may be trying to put stress on you or lower your salary expectations. The best response to this question is to turn it around to your advantage.

I didn't know we were at the stage of discussing the salary question. I really need to know more about the position—duties, responsibilities, expected performance, etc. And I'm not sure you have enough information about me to begin discussing money. I would prefer that we discuss this question later when we have had a chance to get more information on each other. For now, I believe I should be paid what I am worth. I would think you would agree with that concept too, wouldn't you?

If this approach fails and the interviewer persists, take control of the money question by asking several of these questions from **your** perspective:

How much does someone with my qualifications normally receive in your organization? What were you paying the last person? Why would your pay scale be lower than the industry standard? Have others taken pay cuts to join your organization?

■ **How important is job security?**

While job security is important to most people, you should not answer this question by indicating it is your major concern. Focus your answer on your performance —job security comes to those who **earn** it. For example,

I've never really had job security, so I'm not sure what exactly it is. I expect to stay with your company because of my performance and because the company fulfills my career goals. If I'm not meeting your expectations, or if the company doesn't meet my expectation, then I shouldn't be here. I look at a job not for security but for what I can achieve for both the company and myself.

■ **How long do you expect to stay with our company?**

Answer this question in the same manner as the previous question—the bottom line is "as long as both of you are satisfied with the arrangement."

■ **How do you define success?**

This is not the time for deep introspection, nor is it

appropriate to answer from solely a self-centered perspective. Try to tie personal goals to corporate ones.

To me success is accomplishing each day's work on time and on target so that the goals of the company can be met. Of course, the monetary rewards for a job well done are also important so that I can meet my financial obligations.

- **How do you spend your leisure time?**

The employer may be trying to determine whether you are an active person, i.e., likes to camp and hike; a sedentary person, i.e., watch baseball; a joiner, i.e., active in your community's neighborhood watch, or a volunteer, i.e., involved in a food kitchen for indigent persons. Determine what you know about the company and the interviewer. Select from among your interests those you believe best fit the job or the corporate image. Be careful not to mention too many interests though—you must have energy left to do the job!

I really enjoy camping out and hiking when weather permits. It gives me a chance to clear my head of the problems of the work week. I find I return to work on Monday with a clear head and renewed energy.

Career Goals

- **Tell me about your career goals.**

This open-ended question allows you to communicate your goals to the employer. If you have completed a self-assessment and written a resume which included an objective, the answer to this question should be easy. Try to link your skills and abilities to the employer's needs:

My major goal is to move into a management-level position that would enable me to work closely with top management in developing new approaches to marketing our software system in Europe and the Middle East. I believe this company has an excellent product that would do very well in these and other overseas markets. My international marketing background would contribute to opening these markets.

- **What would you like to accomplish during the next 10 years?**

Again, keep your answer employer-centered rather than self-centered. You want to communicate that your goals are in line with those of the employer. For example,

I would like to see 40 percent of the company's sales derived from overseas markets. And I want to play a major role in developing those markets during the next ten years. Indeed, in the year 2002, I want us to look back at this year as being the year in which the company reoriented its marketing program around a truly global perspective.

- **How do your present career goals differ from your career goals 10 years ago?**

Your answer should indicate that you both learn and grow with time. Experience teaches you to alter your goals in the face of new realities. For example,

When I entered this field 10 years ago, I had a very simple goal—work my way up to the top of XYZ Company. However, little did I know how rapidly this field would change in the face of new technology and greater competition. Three years after I started, XYZ Company was bought out by TSR Company in a merger that eventually ended up in bankruptcy for TSR Company. In the meantime, I was hired by two other companies where I moved into middle management positions. I quickly learned my original career goals were unrealistic given the rapidly changing nature of work today. I think my career goals are now more realistic—do what I really love which is to make great quality sound systems. As a result, I'm much happier with my career today than I was five or ten years ago when my career didn't seem to be progressing according to my expectations.

- **Where do you see yourself here five years from now?**

Again, focus on the employer's needs. Whatever you do, don't indicate you hope to be in president's seat which is already occupied. That would be both presumptuous and threatening to others in the organization. For example,

I would hope to be in a position of major responsibility for marketing. I'm not sure what that position is or will be in the future. I feel I have the necessary skills and experience to grow into such a position.

- **Describe a major goal you set for yourself recently.**

  You may select a personal or professional goal, but if you discuss a personal goal you will position yourself better if you can relate it to your professional advancement. *"I want to complete my B.A."* is a personal goal but one that supports your professional advancement. Another one might be *"I want to find a job that is right for me."* Be ready to elaborate on what you are doing to achieve the goal.

- **What are you doing to achieve that goal?**

  Ideally if you are asked a question about your goals such as the one above, you should indicate how you plan to achieve that goal without being asked. It shows you are a purposeful individual who, once you set a goal, will follow through. You have enrolled in an MBA program or this interview is evidence of your job-finding efforts. If you have already received a job offer(s), that would certainly show success.

- **Have you ever thought of switching careers?**

  The interviewer may be asking this question to see if you are committed to your current career and job. It's best to indicate you are not now thinking of changing careers. For example,

  In fact, I did go through a career change seven years ago. I used to be a high school teacher. However, after eight years in the classroom I thought it was time to do something else with my life. In the process

of identifying career alternatives, I conducted a self-assessment in which I learned I was perhaps best suited for a career in sales. It was another form of teaching but in sales I got immediate feedback and saw results. I've never regretted making the change, and I've really enjoyed my last seven years in sales. I plan to continue in sales.

Other Questions

- **Tell me about yourself.**

This is not the time to outline your biography from childhood to the present. Concentrate on your skills and experience, with special reference to accomplishments that relate to the needs of the employer. Talk about your strengths. Anticipate this type of question as you prepare for the interview by listing

- 5 of your outstanding personal qualities as they relate to the work setting.

- 5 of your strongest skills that relate to the job

- 5 positive work related accomplishments

Try to remember the points you have identified so you can respond to this or a similar question, but don't try to memorize what you say about each one—just talk about it naturally to the interviewer.

- **What do you know about our company?**

Of course you have done your research on any company you interview with and you know what they do, how long they have been in business, how large the company is as well as whether they are growing, stagnant, or declining. Your answer should be brief but indicate you do know about them. If you can cite something about the firm that really interests you—so much the better.

I know you are an association promoting wildlife preservation; you celebrate your 25th anniversary this year; you have approximately 2.5 million members and have experienced steady increases in membership each of the past ten years. I am especially impressed with your programs to preserve the northwest spotted egret.

- **What trends do you see in our industry?**

This question too requires that you have done your research. If you have conducted informational interviews, you should have most of the information for answering this question. If not, go online and visit the Web site of the company as well as other firms in the same or related industries. Read journals in the areas of your professional interest as well as business magazines to keep up with the rapid changes taking place.

- **What would be the perfect job for you?**

Your perfect job should relate to the one you are interviewing for as well as to a desirable organizational culture that allows you to do your best. For example,

The perfect job would be one in which I would be allowed to fully use my talents. The job for which I applied may well be such a job. I would hope I would be given an opportunity to work on important projects and eventually given responsibility to head up my own team. I work well in group settings and enjoy taking initiative in developing large and complex projects.

- **What would you change about this position as well as our company?**

Be very careful in answering this question. While you know some things about the company, you probably don't know enough to be so presumptuous as to offer solutions to their problems. After all, changes you propose may negatively affect someone's pet project. You would merely demonstrate your ignorance of the internal dynamics of the organization before you had a chance to settle in to learn how the organization really operates. Be tactful and thoughtful in your response. It's best to indicate you need to learn more about the organization. You are not about to rock the boat before you have had a chance to climb aboard! For example,

I'm sure there are things I might want to change about the position once I begin work. However, I'm not prepared to make any proposals at this time. I usually take some time to learn about the organization and the people I will be working with. I would want to consult those who are most affected by my position to see what they feel needs to be changed. As for changes in the organization, I would hope to give you an answer to that question within a few months. I need to get a firm grasp of how the organization operates as well as learn more about the organizational goals and those I'll be working with.

■ **What type of person would you hire for this position?**

The answer to this question is simple—someone like you who meets the employer's expectations. For example,

I would hire someone who has depth of experience, clear goals, and a proven track record of performance. I also would want to feel comfortable with the person. Without a doubt, I know I would hire myself.

■ **What similarities do you see between this and your current/most recent position?**

Obviously you want to focus on similarities that emphasize the strengths you brought to your current or former position as well as the areas of responsibility that you liked.

■ **What makes this position different from your current/most recent position?**

Focus on areas in which the firm where you are interviewing has an advantage over your present/previous firm. You might say, for example, *"The management team seems more supportive." "The company goals are more in line with my philosophy." "The work is more meaningful (or more challenging.)"*

■ **Have you ever been fired or asked to resign? Why?**

Be careful in how you answer this one—be honest but
not stupid. If you were fired or were asked to resign,
admit it in a different language. And then explain the
circumstances in as positive a manner as possible—
without being negative toward your former employer.
People get fired everyday, often for no fault of their own.
What's important is how to explain the situation. What
have you learned from the experience? For example,

> *Twelve years ago I resigned after meeting with my*
> *employer over several unresolved issues. We both*
> *reached an amiable agreement in which I left volun-*
> *tarily in exchange for three months severance pay.*
> *We had several disagreements, mostly concerning*
> *management policies. We both thought it best that*
> *we part company rather than continue in what was*
> *becoming a difficult situation for both of us. In*
> *looking back, I realize I was young at the time and*
> *thus less willing to listen and compromise. If I were*
> *doing it over today, I would have worked more*
> *closely with my supervisor and attempted to better*
> *understand his point of view rather than try to*
> *persuade him to adopt my proposals. Nonetheless,*
> *we parted on good terms and are still friends today.*
> *I learned a great deal from this experience and know*
> *I'm better for having left that job.*

Other situations differ. For example, you may have been
fired because you refused to follow unethical or illegal
directions:

I was let go at ABC Trucking Company three years ago. I could have stayed, but my supervisor asked me to falsify the accounts to avoid payroll taxes. I refused to do so and was immediately locked out of my office and terminated that same day. This was a difficult period for me financially since I remained unemployed for nearly three months. But I don't regret what I did. Honesty in the workplace is very important to me. No job is worth breaking the law over. In fact, my former employer is now under indictment for tax evasion.

- **How long have you been looking for another job?**

Whatever you do, don't answer this question by indicating you have been looking for a long time. You may sound desperate or incapable of finding work with others. If you have been looking for a while, emphasize how selective you are in settling for a quality employer. For example,

I've been exploring the job market for the past few months. Since I'm looking for something very special that fits my particular interests and skills, yours is only one of very few positions I've seriously considered.

- **Are you willing to relocate?**

You'll have to supply the answer to this question. Obviously, if you are unwilling to relocate and the job requires relocation, don't expect to be considered further for the position. At the same time, you may want to appear "open" on this question, especially if relocation is an option as long as you know where you will be going. Employers today understand the serious implications of relocation for spouses and families. For example,

> *It depends on where I would be required to relocate. I do have a family with a working spouse and school-age children. Since a relocation decision affects them as much as me, this is something I would need to discuss with them. Where would I expect to be relocated and within how long after joining the company? Does the company provide relocation assistance for working spouses?*

- **How many days per month are you willing to travel?**

Again, this is a question only you can answer. Try to find out from the interviewer how often you would be expected to travel. Do this by turning around the question:

> *I'm not sure about the extent of travel involved with this position. How many days per month would I be expected to travel? And where would I normally travel to?*

- **What are your salary expectations?**

Watch out for this question. It should be the very last question you address—**after** you have had a chance to learn about the worth of the position as well as demonstrate your value to the employer. This question is most appropriate for a separate type of job interview—salary negotiation. It should arise after you have a strong indication you will be offered the job. But the interviewer may try to raise it earlier in the interview. You should answer this question in the same manner we suggested you should answer the question about taking a cut in pay. Delay the question or turn it around so the interviewer begins revealing to you his pay range for the position:

What is your pay range for someone in this position with my experience?

If the pay range indicated is compatible with the figures your research has led you to expect, you can put the bottom of your expected salary at the top of the employer's range. For example, if the interviewer indicates that the company's range is $39,000 to $42,000 and this is consistent with your understanding of industry pay, you can either indicate your acceptance of that range or leave yourself some negotiating room for later on in which case you might respond:

My expectation was in the range of $42,000 to $45,000, so we are talking in the same ballpark.

■ **How soon could you begin work?**

If you need to resign from your present job, you may be expected to give at least a two week notice. However, more notice may be expected for high level positions. You might turn the question around by asking

When would you want me to begin work?

If he says immediately, ask for two to four weeks which is a normal time frame for individuals who must leave one job for another one.

You can also expect specific questions relating to your technical expertise, management abilities, and specialized knowledge. These will vary considerably with the position, organization, and individual. For example, if you are interviewing for a computer programming position, you will probably be asked questions about the specific equipment you use, are capable of using, or want to use. If you are interviewing for a management-level position, expect questions relating to "situations" you are likely to encounter, such as how you would deal with a subordinate who by-passes the chain of command in reporting directly to your superiors or who consistently arrives late to work.

Illegal Questions

Title VII of the Civil Rights Act of 1964 makes discrimination on the basis of race, sex, religion, or national origins illegal in personnel decisions. Questions that delve into these areas as well as others, such as age, height, or weight, are also illegal, unless they can be shown to directly relate to bonafide occupational qualifications. Most interviewers are well aware of these restrictions and will not ask you illegal questions. However, you may still encounter such questions either because of ignorance on the part of the interviewer or blatant violation of the regulation. As we noted earlier when discussing "personal" questions, many interviewers may ask these questions indirectly. However, some interviewers still ask them directly.

Women are more likely to face illegal questions than men. Some employers still ask questions regarding birth control, child care, or how their husbands feel about them working or traveling. The following types of questions are considered illegal:

- Are you married, divorced, separated, or single?
- How old are you?
- Do you go to church regularly?
- Do you have many debts?
- Do you own or rent your home?
- What social or political organizations do you belong to?
- What does your spouse think about your career?
- Are you living with anyone?
- Are you practicing birth control?
- Were you ever arrested?
- How much insurance do you have?
- How much do you weigh?
- How tall are you?

Although we hope you will not encounter these types of questions during your job search, you should consider how you would handle them if they arise. Your decision should be thought out carefully beforehand rather than made in the stressful setting of the interview. It must be your decision—one that you feel comfortable with.

You may want to consider the following suggestions as options for handling illegal and personal questions. If you encounter such questions, your choice may depend upon which is more important to you: defending a principle or giving yourself the greatest chance to land the job. You may decide the job is not as important as the principle. Or you may decide, even though you really want this job, you could never work in the organization that employed such clods, and tell them so.

On the other hand, you may decide to answer the question, offensive though it may be, because you really want the job. If you get the job, you vow you will work from within the organization to change such interview practices.

There is yet a third scenario relating to illegal questions. You may believe the employer is purposefully trying to see how you will react to stressful questions. Will you lose your temper or will you answer meekly? Though a rather dangerous practice for employers, this does occur. In this situation you should remain cool and answer tactfully by indicating indirectly that the questions may be inappropriate.

For example, if you are divorced and the interviewer asks about your divorce, you could respond by asking, *"Does a divorce have a direct bearing on the responsibilities of _____?"* If the interviewer asks if you are on the pill, you could respond, *"Yes, I take three pills a day—vitamins A, B, and C, and because of them, I haven't missed a day's work in the past year."* The interviewer should get the message, and you will have indicated you can handle stressful questions.

A possible response to any illegal question—regardless of motive—is to turn what appears to be a negative into a positive. If, for example, you are female and the interviewer asks you how many children you still have living at home and you say, *"I have five—two boys and three girls,"* you can expect this answer will be viewed as a negative. Working mothers with five children at home may be viewed as neither good mothers nor dependable employees. Therefore, you should immediately follow your initial response with a tactful elaboration that will turn this potential negative into a positive. You might say,

I have five—two boys and three girls. They are wonderful children who, along with my understanding husband, take great care of each other. If I didn't have such a supportive and caring family, I would never think of pursuing a career in this field. I do want you to know that I keep my personal

life separate from my professional life. That's very important to me and my family, and I know it's important to employers. In fact, because of my family situation, I make special arrangements with other family members, friends, and day-care centers to ensure that family responsibilities never interfere with my work. But more important, I think being a mother and working full-time has really given me a greater sense of responsibility, forced me to use my time well, and helped me better organize my life and handle stress. I've learned what's important in both my work and life. I would hope that the fact that I'm both a mother and I'm working—and not a working mother—would be something your company would be supportive of, especially given my past performance and the qualifications I would bring to this job.

Here you were able to take both an illegal question and a potential negative and turn them into a positive—perhaps the most tactful and effective way of dealing with a situation other interviewees might respond to in a negative manner.

You should decide before you go into the interview how you will handle similar situations. If you are prepared for possible illegal questions, you may find your answers to such questions to be the strongest and most effective of the interview!

6

Dynamite Answers: The Nonverbal Component

Today most people recognize that **how** they communicate is itself a message. In fact, the nonverbal channel may convey both the bulk of the message and be the most believable. Communication studies suggest that in many situations approximately two thirds of what is communicated is through nonverbal means, and because we know that nonverbal behaviors are the harder to control, we tend to give greater credence to these messages.

The Nonverbal Edge

We also hear from people who conduct screening interviews that the initial decision whether to screen a person out of or into a future interview—made during the first 3-5 minutes of the session —is seldom changed even though the entire interview may be five to ten times that length. What are the interviewers responding to? Certainly not primarily to the content of the verbal interchange, but rather to initial reactions to nonverbal cues.

Thus how you dress for the interview, how well you control the outward signs of nervousness, and how dynamic you are as you talk to the employer will all contribute to the overall impression that will weigh in heavily on the outcome. Strategies to help you be a winner in these areas will be the focus of this chapter.

A Winning Image

Appearance is the first thing you communicate to those you meet. Before you have a chance to speak, others notice your appearance and dress and draw inferences about your character, competence, and capabilities. Image has the greatest impact on the perceptions others have of us when they have little other information on which to base judgments. This is precisely the situation a job applicant finds himself in at the start of an interview.

Many people object to having their capabilities evaluated on the basis of their appearance and dress. *"But that is not fair,"* they argue. *"People should be hired on the basis of their ability to do the job—not on how they look."* But debating the lack of merit or complaining about the unfairness of such behavior does not alter reality. Like it or not, people do make initial judgments about others based on their appearance. Since you cannot alter this fact, it is best to learn to use it to your advantage. If you effectively manage your image, you can convey positive messages regarding your authority, credibility and competence.

Much has been written on how to dress professionally, especially since John Molloy first wrote his books on dressing for success in the 1970's. Although some expectations for dressing have changed in the past decade, for the job interview it is still best to err on the side of conservatism.

Dynamite Images For Men

It is important to know the range of options you have available from the most powerful professional look to a less powerful, but still acceptable business look. The most powerful attire for a male to wear to an interview is a suit. Let's look at power suits in terms of color, fabric, and style. The suit colors that convey the greatest power are navy blue or medium to dark gray. Usually the darker the shade, the greater amount of authority it conveys to the wearer. However, you would do well to avoid black, which in our society is a color for funeral or formal attire; it conveys so much authority as to be threatening to an interviewer. If you want your attire to convey a bit less authority, camel or beige are other acceptable colors for a business suit. Still less power could be conveyed by choosing to wear a sport coat and slacks rather than a suit. Again, you have a range from which to choose and still be within the bounds of acceptable business attire. You must make your choice based on your goals and what you believe to be appropriate to the situation and the job for which you are interviewing. There may be times when you purposefully select this slightly less profession-al—yet acceptable choice and choose not to wear a suit. Remember though, the interviewer expects you will be on your best behavior and this applies to your appearance as well as how you conduct yourself. Most applicants choose to dress as if they were after a job several levels above the one for which they are actually interviewing.

Your suit should be made of a natural fiber. A good blend of a natural fiber with some synthetic is acceptable as long as it has the look of the natural fiber. The very best suit fabrics are wool, wool blends, or fabrics that look like them. Even for the warmer summer months, men can find summer weight wool suits that are comfortable and look good. They are your best buy.

The style of your suit should be classic—well-tailored and well-styled. Avoid suits that appear trendy unless you are applying for a job in a field where being on the forefront of fashion is valued. A conservative suit that has a timeless classic styling will serve you best not only for the interview, but it will give you several years of wear once you land the job. Select a shirt color that is lighter than the color of your suit. White long-sleeved shirts still are most acceptable with a business suit, although many pin stripes are seen in the halls of business today.

A silk tie will look better than other fabrics. Make sure the width is current and select a pattern that goes with the rest of your outfit, looks good on you and is fairly conservative. Dark, classic shoes and dark socks will complete your success look. For more information on business attire for men—updated for the 90's—read *Red Socks Don't Work* by Kenneth Karpinski.

Dynamite Images For Women

Few men would consider wearing anything other than a suit to a job interview—especially an interview for a managerial or professional position. Women are often less certain what is appropriate. The attire that will convey the greatest professionalism, authority and competence is a suit—with a matching skirt and jacket. However, a slightly less powerful look, but one that gets high marks today is to wear a base—skirt and blouse—of one color paired with a jacket of another color. If the skirt and blouse are a solid color the jacket may be a plaid—ideally repeating the blouse and skirt color—as one color of the plaid. This combination conveys the look of a suit, but is more individualistic, slightly less powerful, and very much in style. Dark colors will convey greater power than lighter colors. Gray, navy or camel are conservative, but not your only choices.

Similar to men's suits, your suit should be made of a natural fiber, or a blend of a natural fiber with a synthetic that has the look of the natural fiber. The very best winter-weight suit fabrics are wool or wool blends. For warmer climates or the summer months, women will find few summer weight wool suits made for them. A fabric that has the look of textured silk or silk blend is a good choice.

Your suit style should be classic: well-tailored, well-styled, and avoid trendy looks unless you are certain it is appropriate for the business where you are applying. It is better to err on the side of conservatism—usually better tolerated than a mistake in the other direction. A conservative, classic styled suit will last for years. Indeed, you can afford to buy good quality clothing if you know you can wear it for several seasons.

Buy silk blouses if you can afford them. Keep in mind not only the purchase price of the blouse, but the cleaning bill as well. If you don't buy silk, look for blouse fabrics that have the look and feel of silk. Long sleeved blouses have the greatest power look and necklines should complement the lines of the suit jacket and not be too revealing.

Give your outfit a finished look by accessorizing it effectively. Silk scarves or necklaces that enhance your outfit, but don't call undue attention to themselves can help complete your polished look. A basic pump—dark, if your skirt color is dark—with little or no decoration and a medium heel height is best.

You may choose to carry a purse or attache case, but not both at the same time. It is difficult not to look clumsy trying to handle both a purse and an attache case. One way to carry both is to keep a slim purse with essentials inside the attache case. If you need to go out to lunch, or any place where you choose not to carry the attache case, just pull out your purse and you're off!

Let Nervousness Work For You

Anyone about to face a job interview experiences some nervous anticipation. The degree of nervousness will differ from one person to another, but it is a basic human response to a threatening situation. Most job applicants indicate they wish they could rid themselves of their feelings of nervousness. Although an understandable desire, even if you could do so, the result would be counterproductive.

The feelings you may describe as nervousness—a queasy feeling of "butterflies" in your stomach, sweaty palms, a dry mouth, an increased heartbeat, or knees or hands that tremble—are the physiological manifestations of an increased flow of Adrenalin. This physiological reaction to what you perceive as danger can be just as useful to you as you prepare to "do battle" in the interview as it was to our caveman ancestors who faced a different kind of jungle out there. The caveman when faced with a dangerous situation made a decision to stand his ground and fight or to flee. In either case Adrenalin was his ally and helped him to fight more fiercely or flee more rapidly. It will work for you too if you will learn to manage it rather than trying to fight it.

A limited amount of controlled nervousness will actually keep you on your toes and help you do a better job in the interview than as if you were overconfident and complacent. How can you best manage this nervousness? First, by recognizing it for what it is— an asset—and trying to manage it rather than working against it. Most important, be prepared for the interview. You must do your data gathering on the job field as well as the organization prior to the interview. Anticipate questions you are likely to be asked and formulate your own questions based on information you wish to acquire on the organization. Practice responding to likely questions—not by memorizing answers, but trying to talk through answers in different ways to convey the "jist" or basic content.

Experience is the best teacher, so the more interviews you engage in the better you will become and the more comfortable you will feel. Accept opportunities to interview and critique yourself after each one. Learn from your experience and you will do even better the next time. Leave yourself plenty of time to get to the place of the interview. You do not need the added stress of fearing you will be late because you misjudged the travel time or got into an unexpected traffic tie-up to upset your nerves at the last moment.

Project Composure

As you wait in the outer office to meet with the interviewer, channel your nervous energy productively. Often there are materials about the company on a table along with other reading material. Pick up material about the company and really read it— don't just pretend to. You may learn something about the organization you can comment on or ask questions about in your interview. If nothing about the company is available, pick up a business magazine. Since you are already on display, make your choice of reading material a positive statement about you.

You can better control your nervousness by following advice often given to public speakers. As you walk into the interview room, try to take a few slow deep breaths. If you breathe from your diaphragm, as you should, you can do this subtly so the interviewer will be unaware of it. This should relax you a bit. Although it is easier said than done, the more you can get your mind off yourself and concentrate on the other person, the more comfortable you will feel. Try to be other-directed. Rather than concentrate on your needs and fears, concern yourself with the employer's needs and questions.

The receptionist may direct you to the interviewer or the interviewer may come out to meet you. Either way, stand up to your full height before you take a step. Look alert, forceful, and energetic. If the interviewer comes out to meet you, walk over and shake his or her hand firmly.

If you are sent to a room where the interviewer is standing, walk toward him or her and shake hands. If he or she is seated and does not look up, stand up, or offer a handshake, you should wait a moment and then sit down. However, wait for the interviewer to initiate the conversation.

Project Dynamism

Applicants invited to an employment interview have already been screened in. The employer believes they possess at least the basic qualifications for the job, such as education and work experience. At this point the employer will look for several qualities in the candidates that were not discernable from paper qualifications— credibility, intelligence, competence, spontaneity, friendliness, likability, and enthusiasm. In the end, employers hire people whom they like and believe will interact well on an interpersonal basis with the rest of the staff.

Your enthusiasm is one of the most important qualities you can convey. In fact, studies indicate that three major components define credibility: expertise, trustworthiness, and dynamism. The first two components we can all relate to readily. We know we must be perceived as competent and honest. But dynamism— that's news to many job seekers. What it means is that you need to be a dynamic individual who exudes enthusiasm and drive. A dynamic person is more believable than one who comes across in a flat, low key manner. He also conveys the impression that he is a doer, someone who can get things done. So you need to let your enthusiasm show. Granted this can be overdone, but try to project yourself in a dynamic manner.

The following are some behaviors that will reinforce what you say in a positive and dynamic way.

- **Lean slightly into the interview**. If you sit with a slight forward lean toward the interviewer it communicates your interest in what the interviewer is saying as well as in the interview proceedings. Your forward lean should be so slight as to be almost imperceptible. Be careful not to overdo this. You do not want it to be so obvious the behavior calls attention to itself.

- **Make frequent eye contact with the interviewer(s)**. Eye contact establishes rapport with the interviewer. You appear interested in what is being said and you will be perceived as more trustworthy if you will look at the interviewer as you ask and answer questions. To say someone has "shifty eyes" or cannot "look us in the eye" is to imply they may not be completely honest. To have a direct, though moderate eye gaze, in our culture conveys interest as well as trustworthiness.

- **Project a pleasant facial expression**. A face that appears alive and interested conveys a positive attitude. You should smile enough to convey your positive attitude, but not so much that you will not be taken seriously. Some people naturally smile often and others hardly ever smile. Monitor your behavior or ask a friend to give you feed-back. Certainly your facial expression should be compatible with what is being discussed, and smiling inanely all the time is not to be encouraged. Ideally your face should reflect honest interest in the dynamics of the interview.

Give the interviewer facial feedback rather than an expressionless deadpan.

- **Convey interest and enthusiasm through your vocal inflections.** Though not a visual component, vocal inflection is a critical element of nonverbal communication. Your tone of voice says a lot about you and how interested you are in the interviewer and the organization. Your voice is one of the greatest projectors of dynamism available to you. Use it effectively both in the face-to-face interview and in a telephone interview.

Project Class and Competence

The way you stand, sit and walk—essentially how you carry yourself—has a bearing on how others perceive you. John Molloy is convinced that the "look" that impresses interviewers the most is the upper class carriage—the look of class.

Even if your background is not upper class, as a youngster you were probably prodded by someone in your family to improve how you stood, sat, or walked. Comments such as: *"Keep your shoulders back"* or *"Keep your head erect"* or *"Don't slouch"* were good advice. Too bad some of us didn't listen. If you did not pay much attention to it then, it would be to your advantage to do so now. The look of class and competence includes the following behaviors:

- Keep your shoulders back.
- Keep your head erect.
- Avoid folding your arms across your chest.
- Avoid sitting or standing with arms or legs far apart in what could be described as an "open" position.

- Use gestures that enhance your verbal message.
- Nod your head affirmatively at appropriate times—but do not overdo it.
- Project your voice loudly enough to be heard.
- Articulate clearly—do not mumble.
- Use good diction.
- Use pauses for emphasis.
- Watch your pace—avoid talking too fast or too slowly. Many nervous people tend to talk rapidly.

Perhaps as much as anything, people with class always make the other person feel comfortable. Wait a minute, you say, I'm the one who is uncomfortable. Perhaps, but focus your attention away from yourself. Give your attention to the other person and you may be surprised how well the interview can go.

> **Give your attention to the other person and you will be surprised how well the interview will go.**

If you concentrate on what is being said rather than how you are doing, you will most likely create a good impression on the interviewer. Being other-directed with your nonverbal communication will make you seem more likable and competent than many other candidates who remain self centered and nervous throughout the interview.

7

Dynamite Questions You Should Ask

Even with the best interviewer, you will need to ask questions. Remember, you have a decision to make too. Are you really interested in the job? Does it fit your goals and skills? Will it give you the chance to do something you do well and enjoy doing? Will it give you the opportunity to move in some of the directions you want to move? Use the interview situation to probe areas that will provide answers to these and other questions that are critical to your future.

Ask Questions

When should I ask questions? What questions should I ask? How often should I ask a question? These are some of the concerns of applicants preparing for a job interview. For the most part there are no hard and fast answers—each situation is different. However, there are some guidelines that should help you as you try to analyze your particular interview situation. Some authors have suggested that the applicant ask questions about 10 percent of the time—wait until the interviewer has asked about nine questions and then it is your turn. This advice seems a bit contrived. The interview should be an interchange of questions and answers from both parties. Both have decisions to make and need information to help them evaluate where they want to go from here vis-a-vis the other.

Normally the framework and the flow of the job interview is determined by the employer. As the interview progresses there are likely to be points at which something the interviewer has said raises a question in your mind. If it makes sense to ask the question at this juncture, go ahead. If your question takes up something mentioned by the interviewer, this will most likely follow the flow and not disrupt the pace of the interview. If you are a sensitive listener you should be able to determine whether a question will be well received by the interviewer. Normally near the end of the interview, most employers will ask an applicant if there are any questions he has that have not been answered. At this point you have the opportunity to ask questions that have not been raised as part of the ongoing dynamics of the interview.

What kinds of questions you should ask as well as those that you should not raise—at least not until you have been offered the job—are the focus of this chapter.

Questions About the Company

We assume you have researched the company prior to going for the interview. You already have information gathered from corporate publications and, if the company is a large one, from business directories found in your local library. You went online and checked out the company's Web site. You have talked with employees and former employees in the community to get a handle on the human dimension of working within this company. So you should not have to ask basic questions about what the company does, or the size of the company—either in terms of assets or number of employees. To ask questions about matters that you should have been able to find out from a bit of basic research wastes valuable interview time that could be better spent on other issues and does not impress the interviewer with your resourcefulness.

Questions you might want to ask about the company would revolve around areas not likely covered in materials you could have read previous to your interview. You want to know something about the

- Stability of the position and firm.
- Opportunities available for advancement.
- Management and decision-making styles—teams, hierarchies, degree of decentralization.
- Degree of autonomy permitted and entrepreneurship encouraged.
- Organizational culture.
- Internal politics.

Your questions may cover some of the following areas of inquiry:

- Why is this position open? Is it a new position? If not, why did the person who held it previously leave? If the person was promoted, what position does that person now hold?

- How important is this position to the organization?

- To what extent does the company promote from within versus hiring from the outside?

- What plans for expansion (or cutbacks) are in the immediate future? What effect will these plans have on the position or the department in which it is located?

- On the average, how long do most employees stay with this company?

- Tell me about what it's really like working here in terms of the people, management practices, work loads, expected performance, and rewards.

- How would you evaluate the financial soundness and growth potential of this company?

- If you had to briefly describe this organization, what would you say? What about it's employees? Its managers and supervisors? Its performance evaluation system? Its promotion practices?

- If you had to do it all over again, would you have made the same decision to join this organization? Why?

- Assuming my work is excellent, where do you see me in another five years within this organization?

These are not necessarily the exact questions you may want to ask. For example, if yesterday's paper mentions downsizing plans at the company, then directly to a question as to how that will affect the job and department. Also, this is not an exhaustive list of all the company related questions you may need to ask pertinent to your situation. These questions should provide you with a starting point from which to devise the questions you need to ask.

Questions About the Job

Your questions about the company were designed to get a sense of where the company is headed and perhaps its corporate philosophy. Questions about the job will relate more specifically to the day-to-day activities you could expect if you were to join this organization. You may wish to ask about some of the following concerns.

- How did this opening occur? Is it a newly created position or did someone recently leave the position?

- Tell me about the nature of the work I would be doing most of the time.

- What kinds of peripheral tasks would likely take up the balance of my time?

- What would be my most important duties? Responsibilities?

- What types of projects would I be involved with?

- What kinds of clients would I be working with?

- What changes is management interested in having take place with the direction of this department?

- What is the management style of the person who would be my supervisor?

- In what ways is management looking for this function

(the function performed by the department you would be working in) to be improved?

- What have been the major problems (barriers to reaching department goals) in the past?

- What will be the major challenges for the person who is hired?

- How often will I be expected to travel?

Not all of these questions may relate to your specific situation, and you may be able to formulate many others that do. Use this listing as a guide to the type of information you may need to better determine whether this job would be a good fit with your skills, the way you like to work, and your goals.

Questions About the Work Environment

How happy you will be in a job involves more than the work you will be doing. The people you will be working with, the way your performance is evaluated, and the support the company gives its employees in terms of training and development are issues that will affect how you feel about the organization once you are on the job. Consider asking questions that relate to some of these areas of concern.

- Can you tell me something about the people I would be working with? Working for?

- How is performance evaluated? How often, by whom, what criteria are used? Does the employee have input into the evaluation? Do you have an annual performance appraisal system in place? How long has it been operating? How does it relate to promotions and salary increments? How do employees feel about this system? What changes do you feel need to be made in the system?

- Can you tell me something about the company's management system? How do supervisors see their role in this company? Tell me about my immediate supervisor.

- Is there much internal politics that would affect my position? Will I be expected to become part of anyone's group? How controversial is this hiring decision? Would you say all employees feel they are dealt with fairly by management? Who is considered the most powerful or influential in my division?

- Does the company provide in-house training? Does it support employees taking advantage of outside training in areas where it does not provide training programs? Is there support for employees returning to school for additional formal education?

- How open are opportunities for advancement? Assuming high performance, to what other positions might I progress?

Questions to Ask At the Close

Assuming the interview has progressed to its final stage and you have asked questions about the organization, the job, and the work environment, you may breathe a sigh of relief. But you are not finished yet. Remember, you need to ask questions that will establish what you do from here. You do not want to go home and wait for weeks hoping to hear about this job.

Assuming you are still interested in the job, tell that to the interviewer. Ask when she (or the management team) expects to make a decision and when you could expect to hear. Then take the date a day or two after she has indicated a decision should be reached and ask, *"If I haven't heard from you by ___(date)___, may I call you?"* Almost always the interviewer will indicate you may call. Mark the date on your calendar and make certain you do call if you have not heard by then.

This is also a good time to ask the employer if there is any other information they need in order to act on your application. If you still have questions concerning the job, you may want to ask the interviewer if there are two or three present or former employees you might talk to about the organization. He should provide you with the names and phone numbers. Be sure to contact them.

Questions About Salary and Benefits

The employer may bring up the salary and benefits issues earlier, but you should avoid asking benefits related questions until you are offered the job. This means, that even though it is of great interest to you, you withhold asking questions about salary, vacation time, sick leave, working hours, medical insurance and any other benefits issues. There will be time for that if you get the job offer. Of course, if the employer raises these issues, you may ask questions in response to what he has raised. But even then avoid letting this area become the all-consuming focus of discussion prior to the job offer.

After you have been offered the job, you should ask benefits related questions. If it has not already been discussed, you will want to ask about the salary range for the position. Try to talk in terms of a **range** rather than a single salary figure. Discussing a range will give greater flexibility for some negotiation. Usually there is room for some negotiation in arriving at a salary. Your research on the field—especially information gained from informational interviews—should give you an indicator of what the going market rate is for the job in question. Thus you should know whether the figure or range quoted is at the low, high, or mid range and decide whether to accept it or attempt to negotiate a higher figure. For further information on negotiating salary, you may wish to look at one of our other books, ***Dynamite Salary Negotiations***, which is also published by Impact Publications.

You may wish to ask how often salaries are reviewed. Starting at the high end of the salary scale for your industry may not seem like nearly such a good deal when after three years on the job you still haven't received an increase. You will probably wish to know how salary increases are determined—annual cost-of-living increases, a merit system, or a combination of both. How large are the increases on average?

You'll probably want to establish what other benefits the company offers. Large companies may offer both a plan for term life insurance and medical insurance. You may wish to probe what deductible the medical insurance covers as well as whether the employer pays the entire cost or only a portion of the cost of health insurance. Many companies will pay the health insurance cost for the employee only. The employee must pay the additional cost for family coverage. As the cost of medical plans continue to rise, employers often require the employee to pay a greater portion of the cost of insurance than was once the case. Smaller companies may or may not have insurance plans to cover employees.

Larger companies are more likely to have retirement plans than smaller organizations. It is reasonable to inquire whether there is a retirement plan and how it is structured. Do you have to spend the rest of your life with the company before you are vested? Some large companies may offer profit sharing plans to employees.

You will probably want to know about the leave policy. Some organizations designate a certain number of days each year for sick leave; others offer leave designated as numbers of days of sick leave and days of personal leave. How many paid holidays employees get each year as well as vacation days are likely to be benefits of interest to most applicants.

More and more large organizations are also providing day care opportunities for employees' children. Some companies give employees a choice of employer paid benefits, but may not make all available as fully paid by the company. For example, many two-career couples do not need health insurance provided by both employers. One may choose company paid health insurance through one spouse's employer and the other may select a paid day care arrangement through his.

Smaller firms may not be able to offer many of the benefits mentioned above, but nonetheless may offer attractive employment opportunities. Questions about benefits should be raised prior to your acceptance of a job offer.

Questions About Relocation

If accepting a job offer involves your making a move to a new community, you need to determine what moving expenses your employer will pay. The most generous can include the cost of shipping your household goods to the new community; a per diem to cover hotel accommodations and food for travel days and perhaps a week or two after arrival in the new community while waiting for your household shipment to arrive; a portion of the closing costs on the home you are buying in the community, and even a guaranteed sale of your house in the community you are leaving. However, as the economy tightens, you are likely to find fewer employers able or willing to subsidize your move to this extent and more and more job applicants willing to accept employment without these subsidies. In many cases, all the expenses of a community move may be yours to pay. But whatever the case, you need to have a clear understanding of who will pay which expenses before you make your decision whether to accept the job.

Be sure you have a realistic estimate of the cost of living in the new community before you accept a position as well as prior to negotiating your salary. What appears to be a large salary increase over your present or most previous job may actually be the equivalent to a cut in pay if you are moving from a town in the midwest to southern California, New York City, Boston, or the Washington, D.C. metro area.

For more information on questions to ask at a job interview, see Richard Fein's *101 Dynamite Questions to Ask At Your Job Interview* (Impact Publications).

8

Dynamite Follow-Ups

The interview is not over until you or someone else has been offered and accepted the job. The fact that you conducted an interview or a series of interviews with an employer should not give you pause to relax. If you really want this job, you should focus on doing several things during the post-interview period. While you closed the interview once, when you left the interview site, you need to further close it through post-interview activities that will maintain the attention and interest of the employer.

It's Not Over Until It's Over

Once the interview is over, you still have work to do. This is not the time to sit back and wait to be called. For starters, as soon as possible after each interview and while it is fresh in your mind, record information about the encounter that you can review later. Try to be as specific as possible: list everything from the name of the person(s) you spoke with to the data you gathered regarding the position and organization; your skills that particularly fit the job requirements; and when the employer indicated the next decision would be made. This is also a good time to mark the date when you will place your follow-up call on your calendar.

Next, write a nice thank you letter, similar to our example on page 175. Express your appreciation to the employer for a good interview. Indicate your continued interest in the position, assuming this is the case, and briefly summarize your skills as they relate to the position. Close by indicating you are waiting to hear from her on X date—use the date she indicated she would have made her decision. Keep this letter focused and brief. The employer is a busy person and is not likely to appreciate nor read a lengthy letter. Keep in mind that though it is a thank you letter, it is a business letter. It should be produced on a typewriter or generated on a letter quality printer using good quality business-size stationery and mailed in a No. 10 business envelope.

At the very least, sending a thank you letter is a courteous thing to do. However, you may get more mileage out of it than just doing the right thing. When your letter arrives, it will remind the interviewer of your candidacy. The brief summation of your skills as they relate to the job focuses her attention on the fit between you and the position. You have also reminded her that you expect to hear from her by a particular date. And if by chance you are one of few to send a thank you letter, you will have set yourself apart from the crowd.

Keep the Process Going

During the days that you are awaiting word from this employer, continue to network and apply for other positions that interest you. You need to continue to actively pursue jobs that fit your goals and skills. The time between an interview and a hiring decision may be weeks. Use this time constructively to promote your job search.

If you do not hear from the employer by the date specified, you must follow through and make the call to inquire whether a decision has yet been made. If they have not made a decision yet, your call will again put you in their minds and this may put you a few points ahead of others under consideration. Your dedication and follow-through will probably score a few more points in your favor. While follow-up alone will not get you the job, if it is a close decision and you call and the other candidate does not, your follow-up phone call could be your ticket to winning the job!

Follow-up Means You Follow-Through

Do both yourself and the employer a favor. If you asked if it would be okay to call the employer in regards to the hiring decision, make sure you do. Too often individuals learn the importance of follow-up, but they only take it to the stage of seeking permission to follow-up or they state they will call at a particular time. But when the time comes, they either forget to do so or they get cold feet and decide not to make that critical telephone call. If you said you would follow-up on a particular date, make sure you do. Your follow-up actions will indicate to the employer that you are someone who also follows through in doing what you say you will do.

If you call and are told the decision has not been made, ask when you might hear from the employer and if it would be okay to call again in another few days. If, on the other hand, the decision has been made and you were not chosen, write another thank you letter, similar to the example on page 176, in which you express your disappointment in not being chosen. Sincerely express your appreciation for the opportunity to interview for the position and indicate your continuing interest in working with the employer. You may later discover this thoughtful letter will lead to another job offer. Chances are you will be remembered by the employer as a thoughtful person. And in the end, that is what the job search and interview are all about—being remembered as someone who should be offered the job. Make sure you follow through your follow-up in a manner that will get you remembered for future reference.

If you are offered the job, you also should write a thank you letter, similar to the one on page 177, in which you express your appreciation for the confidence given to you. This can be a very effective thank you letter. It sets an important stage for developing a new and hopefully productive relationship in the coming months and years. It helps relieve the anxiety of the employer who may still be uncertain about his hiring choice.

In the end, how well you conducted the interview, including the quality of your presentation during this immediate post-interview phase, will set the stage in determining how well you will do on the job. The simple courtesy of a thank you letter is the right thing to do for both personal and professional reasons. It will help you get off on the right foot to continued career success with this new employer.

POST-JOB INTERVIEW THANK YOU LETTER

19932 Thornton Drive
Chester, GA 30019
April 9, 19___

David Norton, Director
Marketing Department
SERVICE INTERNATIONAL
1009 State Street
Atlanta, GA 31010

Dear Mr. Norton:

Thank you again for the opportunity to interview for the marketing position. I appreciated your hospitality and enjoyed meeting you and members of your staff.

The interview convinced me of how compatible my background, interests, and skills are with the goals of Service International. My prior marketing experience with the Department of Commerce has prepared me to take a major role in developing both domestic and international marketing strategies. I am confident my work for you will result in considerably expanding the Pacific markets within the next two years.

For more information on the new product promotion program I mentioned, call David Garrett at the Department of Commerce. His number is 202/726-0132. I talked to Dave this morning and mentioned your interest in this program.

I look forward to hearing from you on April 25th.

Sincerely,

Margaret Adams

Margaret Adams

JOB REJECTION FOLLOW-UP LETTER

564 Court Street
St. Louis, MO 53167

September 21, 19___

Ralph Ullman, President
S.T. Ayer Corporation
6921 Southern Blvd.
St. Louis, MO 53163

Dear Mr.. Ullman:

I appreciated your consideration for the Research Associate position. While I am disappointed in not being selected, I learned a great deal about your company, and I enjoyed meeting with you and your staff. I felt particularly good about the professional manner in which you conducted the interview.

Please keep me in mind for future consideration. I have a strong interest in your company. I believe we would work well together. I will be closely following the progress of your organization over the coming months. Perhaps we will be in touch with each other at some later date.

Best wishes.

Sincerely,

Martin Tollins

Martin Tollins

JOB OFFER ACCEPTANCE LETTER

7694 James Court
San Francisco, CA 94826

June 7, 19___

Judith Greene
Vice President
West Coast Airlines
2400 Van Ness
San Francisco, CA 94829

Dear Ms. Greene:

I am pleased to accept your offer, and I am looking forward to joining you and your staff next month.

The customer relations position is ideally suited to my background and interests. I assure you I will give you my best effort in making this an effective position within your company.

I understand I will begin work on July 1. If, in the meantime, I need to complete any paper work or take care of other matters, please contact me.

I enjoyed meeting with you and your staff and appreciated the professional manner in which the hiring was conducted.

Sincerely,

Joan Kitter

Joan Kitter

9

101 Answers You Should Formulate

Reading through examples of response strategies and answers to interview questions based on the point of view of the employer is a good start toward an effective interview, but your hard work should begin now. You need to take these questions and formulate answers that are your own.

Prepare For the 101

A basic key to a successful interview is preparation. Even though you can never predict every question you will be asked, in most instances you can accurately predict 95% or more of the questions you must respond to. Most, perhaps all, of these questions will be similar in intent to the 101 questions found here. As you anticipate how you would respond if you encounter each of these questions in an interview, remember that you are formulating your strategy for a response. You should not try to formulate the exact words you would use and then memorize them. To do this would be a big mistake. At best your answer would likely sound memorized and you would greatly diminish your credibility. At worst, you might forget your memorized response in the middle of your answer.

So consider your answers in terms of basic strategies. What do you hope to convey as you respond to each question? Your goal is to convince the interviewer that you should be offered the job. So as you respond think in terms of the needs of the employer. How do your goals fit with her business needs? Keep this basic tenet in mind as you formulate your strategies in responding to questions you are asked. Try to make time prior to the interview to actually talk through your answers to questions. You may practice answering interview questions (which you have made into a list) posed by a friend or family member or you can read each question and then respond. Practice talking your answers into a tape recorder. Play back the tape and evaluate how you sound.

- Do you sound confident?
- Do you sound dynamic?
- Do you talk in a conversational style? (rather than your response sounding like a "canned" memorized answer)
- Do you speak without excessive fillers such as *"ah"*, *"and ah"*, *"like"* and *"you know"*?
- Do you sound believable?

Each time you talk through an answer your words will be somewhat different since you have purposely not tried to memorize your response. You have thought through strategy of your response, the "jist" of the message you want to convey, but you have not attempted to commit a response to memory.

Additional Questions

You may not be asked any questions beyond ones similar to the 101 interview questions in this chapter. If the questions you are asked do go beyond these they will most likely fall into one of two categories:

- Specific questions that relate to special knowledge or skills required for the job for which you are being considered.

- Questions that are raised by unusual items or unexplained gaps or omissions on your resume or application.

Look over your resume. Is there anything that stands out? If you spent your junior year abroad—not in Paris or Spain—but in Timbuktu or your first job was in Inner Mongolia, these points are likely to raise questions simply because they are unusual choices. The interviewer is going to be curious about your experiences as well as what these choices say about you. If you have a two-year unexplained gap in your job history, this gap is bound to raise the question of what you were doing during this time. You need to be ready with honest, yet positive answers that will further promote your candidacy rather than knock you out of the running. If you have thoughtfully considered your responses and practiced responding with the jist of the message you want to convey, these questions should not throw you. However, if you haven't given such questions much thought your responses are likely to show it.

Few questions should ever be answered with just a *"yes"* or *"no"*. Remember to provide examples as often as possible to support the points you make. If asked by the interviewer whether you are a self-starter you could simply respond *"yes"*. However you score few points for this response. It really says nothing except either that you think you are a self-starter or you think this is the response the interviewer wants to hear. But if you follow your *"yes"* response with an example or two of what you did that demonstrates you were a self-starter in your last job (or in college if you have just graduated and have little work experience) you start to sell yourself. You want to impress the interviewer and you want to stand out from the rest of the applicants being interviewed. Remember to use examples and use them frequently. The examples you use to support the assertions you make help to sell "you" to the interviewer. Examples make what you say about your skills and achievements more clear, more interesting, more credible, and more likely to be remembered.

We are hearing these days about increased use of behavior based and situational interviewing on the part of employers. "Behavior based" means that the interviewer asks you to describe how you responded when you faced an actual situation. "Situational based" questions don't ask for an actual situation, but ask you to imagine a situation and describe how you would act if that occurred. These types of interview questions are an attempt to get applicants to do what they should be doing anyway: expanding their answers with examples that support the assertions they are making.

The questions which follow have already been discussed in previous chapters. If you need to review our suggested strategies just refer to the pages noted. Otherwise try out your best response using a tape recorder. Then listen to your recorded responses and critique them.

Some of the questions may be phrased slightly differently on this list than in the text. Get used to listening for the "jist" of the question—not the exact words. Your interviewers will be trying to ferret out much of the information suggested here, but they will ask the questions in a variety of ways.

Questions About You—Personality/Motivation

1. Why should we hire you? (**page 127**)

2. Are you a self-starter? (**page 126**)

3. What is your greatest strength? (**page 112**)

4. What is your greatest weakness? (**page 113**)

5. What would you most like to improve about yourself? (**page 114**)

6. What are some of the reasons for your success? (**page 114**)

7. Describe your typical work day. (**page 115**)

8. Do you anticipate problems or do you react to them? (**page 117**)

9. How do you deal with stressful situations? (**page 117**)

10. Do you ever lose your temper? (**page 117**)

11. How well do you work under deadlines? (**page 119**)

12. What contributions did you make to your last (or present) company? (**page 119**)

13. What will you bring to this position that another candidate won't? (**page 121**)

14. How well do you get along with your superiors? (**page 122**)

15. How well do you get along with your co-workers? **(page 122)**

16. How do you manage your subordinates? **(page 122)**

17. How do you feel about working with superiors who may have less education than you? **(page 123)**

18. Do you prefer working alone or with others? **(page 123)**

19. How do others view your work? **(page 124)**

20. How do you deal with criticism? **(page 124)**

21. Do you consider yourself to be someone who takes greater initiative than others? **(page 125)**

22. Do you consider yourself a risk-taker? **(page 125)**

23. Are you a good time manager? **(126)**

24. How important is job security? **(page 132)**

25. How do you define success? **(page 132)**

26. How do you spend your leisure time? **(page 133)**

27. What would be the perfect job for you? **(page 138)**

28. What really motivates you to perform on the job? **(page 128)**

29. How old are you? **(page 146)**

30. What does your spouse think about your career? **(page 146)**

31. Are you living with anyone? **(page 146)**

32. Do you have many debts? **(page 146)**

33. Do you own or rent your home? **(pages 97 & 146)**

34. What social or political organizations do you belong to? **(Page 146)**

Questions About Education and On-Going Learning

35. Why didn't you go to college? **(page 104)**

36. Why didn't you finish college? **(page 105)**

37. Why did you select _____ college? **(page 98)**

38. Why did you major in _____? **(pages 90 & 99)**

39. What was your minor in school? **(page 98)**

40. How did your major relate to the work you have done since graduation? **(page 104)**

41. Why weren't your grades better in school? **(page 100)**

42. What subjects did you enjoy most? **(page 98)**

43. What subjects did you enjoy least? **(page 98)**

44. If you could go back and do it over again, what would you change about your college education? (**pages 99 & 103**)

45. What extracurricular activities did you participate in during college? (**page 101**)

46. Tell me about your role in <u>(one of your extracurricular activities)</u>. (**page 101**)

47. What leadership positions did you hold in college? (**page 101**)

48. How does your degree prepare you for the job at _____? (**page 102**)

49. Did you work part-time or full-time while you were in college? (**page 101**)

50. Are you planning to take additional courses or start graduate school over the next year or two? (**page 103**)

51. If you had a choice of several short training sessions to attend, which 2 or 3 would you select? (**page 104**)

52. What materials do you read regularly to keep up with what is going on in your field? (**page 104**)

53. What is the most recent skill you have learned? (**page 105**)

54. What are your educational goals over the next few years? (**page 104**)

Questions About Experience

55. Why do you want to leave your present job or previous jobs? **(pages 91 & 129)**

56. Why have you changed jobs so frequently? **(page 129)**

57. Why would you be more likely to stay here? **(page 129)**

58. What are your qualifications for this job? **(page 106)**

59. What experience prepares you for this job? **(page 107)**

60. What did you like most about your present/most recent job? **(page 107)**

61. What did you like least about your present/most recent job? **(page 108)**

62. What did you like most about your present/most recent boss? **(page 109)**

63. What did you like least about your present/most recent boss? **(page 110)**

64. Tell me about an on-going responsibility in your current/most recent job that you enjoyed. **(page 115)**

65. How does your present job (or most recent) relate to the overall goals of your department/the company? **(page 111)**

66. What has your present/most recent supervisor(s) criticized about your work? **(page 118)**

67. What duties in your present/most recent job do you find it difficult to do? **(page 115)**

68. Why do you want to leave your present job? Are you being forced out? **(page 129)**

69. Why should we hire someone like you—with your experience and motivation? **(page 127)**

70. What type of person would you hire for this position? **(page 140)**

71. Have you ever been fired or asked to resign? **(page 141)**

72. What was the most important contribution you made on your last job? **(page 119)**

73. What do you wish you had accomplished in your present/most recent job but were unable to? **(page 120)**

74. What is the most important thing you've learned from the jobs you've held? **(page 127)**

Your Career Goals

75. Tell me about yourself. **(page 137)**

76. Tell me about your career goals. **(page 133)**

77. What would you like to accomplish during the next 5 years (or ten years). **(page 134)**

78. How do your career goals today differ from your career goals 5 years ago? **(page 134)**

79. Where do you see yourself 5 years from now? **(page 135)**

80. Describe a major goal you set for yourself recently? **(page 135)**

81. What are you doing to achieve that goal? **(page 136)**

82. Have you ever thought of switching careers? **(page 136)**

83. How does this job compare to what would be the perfect job for you? **(page 138)**

84. What would you change about our company to make this your ideal workplace? **(page 139)**

85. How long have you been looking for another job? **(page 142)**

Questions About Why You Want the Job You Are Interviewing For

86. What do you know about our company? **(page 137)**

87. What trends do you see in our industry? **(page 138)**

88. Why do you want to work for us? **(page 128)**

89. How much business would you bring to our firm? **(page 117)**

90. What similarities do you see between this and your current/ most recent position? **(page 140)**

91. What makes this position different from your current/most recent position? **(140)**

92. Why are you willing to take a job you are over-qualified for? **(page 130)**

93. Why are you willing to take a pay cut from your previous (present) position? **(page 131)**

94. What would you change about this position? **(page 139)**

95. How long would you expect to stay with our company? **(page 132)**

96. How do you feel about working overtime or on week-ends? **(page 118)**

97. Are you willing to relocate? **(page 142)**

98. How much are you willing to travel? **(page 143)**

99. What are your salary expectations? **(page 143)**

100. How soon could you begin work? **(page 144)**

101. Do you have any questions?

The answer to this final question is *"Yes, I have a few additional questions."* No matter how thorough the interview, no matter how much give-and-take, you should have at least a question or two—probably more—to ask near the end of the interview. Prepare questions to ask as you prepare for the interview. Having no questions to ask will hurt your chances of getting the job offer. As a result of your conversation with the interviewer, other questions will probably come to mind as the interview progresses. When asked whether you have questions you may indicate that many have been answered thus far, but you have a few additional questions. You should have jotted some questions down as you prepared for your interview. Feel free to refer to that list if you need to at this point. The fact that you have given thought to this aspect of the interview and have come prepared will be viewed as a positive by the interviewer. You may have questions about the relationship of this job to other significant functional areas in the firm; staff development; training programs; career advancement opportunities; the extent to which promotions are from within the organization; how employee performance is evaluated; or the expected growth of the company. You may want to ask questions that probe areas that were touched on earlier during the interview. For example, if the interviewer has mentioned that the company has an excellent training program, you may have specific questions: what kinds of training would you be offered? How frequently? How long do most training programs last?

By all means if you are still interested in this job, before you leave the interview summarize the strong points you would bring to the position and indicate your continued interest in the job and the company. Ask what the next step will be and when they expect to make a decision. Follow the advice in Chapter 7 on the close to the interview and Chapter 8 on the follow up to the interview.

The Authors

Caryl Rae Krannich, Ph.D., and Ronald L. Krannich, Ph.D., operate Development Concepts Incorporated, a training, consulting, and publishing firm. Both are former university professors, high school teachers, management trainers, and consultants. Caryl has served as personnel manager for a newspaper in Florida as well as placement coordinator for a temporary employment agency in Ohio. Ron also is a former Peace Corps Volunteer and Fulbright Scholar. The Krannichs have completed numerous research and technical assistance projects on management, career development, local government, population planning, and rural development during the past 20 years. Their articles appear in major academic journals.

The Krannichs also are two of America's leading career and travel writers. They are authors of twenty-seven career books and eleven travel books. Their career books focus on key job search skills, military and civilian career transitions, government and international careers, travel jobs, and nonprofit organizations. Their body of work represents one of today's most comprehensive collections of career writing. Their books are widely available in bookstores, libraries, and career centers. Many of their works on key job search skills are available interactively on CD-ROM (*The Ultimate Job Source*).

Ron and Caryl continue to pursue their international interests through their innovative *"Treasures and Pleasures...Best of the Best"* series. When not found at their home and business in Virginia, they are probably somewhere in Europe, Asia, Africa, the Middle East, the South Pacific, or the Caribbean pursuing their other passion— researching and writing about quality arts and antiques.

Index

Career Resources

C ontact Impact Publications for a free annotated listing of career resources or visit their World Wide Web site for a complete listing of career resources: *http://www.impactpublications.com.*
The following career resources are available directly from Impact Publications. Complete this form or list the titles, include postage (see formula at the end), enclose payment, and send your order to:

IMPACT PUBLICATIONS
9104-N Manassas Drive
Manassas Park, VA 20111-2366
Tel. 703/361-7300 or Fax 703/335-9486
E-mail: impactp@impactpublications.com

Orders from individuals must be prepaid by check, moneyorder, Visa, MasterCard, or American Express. We accept telephone and fax orders.

Qty.	TITLES	Price	TOTAL

Key Directories/Reference Works

Qty.	TITLES	Price	TOTAL
____	American Almanac of Jobs and Salaries	20.00	____
____	Dictionary of Occupational Titles	39.95	____
____	Directory of Executive Recruiters 1997	44.95	____
____	Directory of Federal Jobs and Employers	21.95	____
____	Occupational Outlook Handbook	16.95	____
____	Professional's Job Finder	18.95	____

Finding Great Jobs and Careers

Qty.	TITLES	Price	TOTAL
____	Best Jobs For the 1990s and Into the 21st Century	19.95	____
____	Change Your Job, Change Your Life	17.95	____
____	Five Secrets to Finding a Job	12.95	____
____	Guide to Internet Job Searching	14.95	____
____	Hoover's Top 2,500 Employers	22.95	____

195

____	How to Get Your Dream Job Using the Web	34.99	_____
____	How to Get Interviews From Classified Job Ads	14.95	_____
____	How to Succeed Without a Career Path	13.95	_____
____	Jobs and Careers With Nonprofit Organizations	15.95	_____
____	What Color Is Your Parachute? 1997	16.95	_____

Cover Letters

____	175 High-Impact Cover Letters	10.95	_____
____	201 Dynamite Job Search Letters	19.95	_____
____	201 Killer Cover Letters	16.95	_____
____	201 Winning Cover Letters for $100,000+ Jobs	24.95	_____
____	Cover Letters For Dummies	12.99	_____
____	Cover Letters That Knock 'Em Dead	10.95	_____
____	Dynamite Cover Letters	14.95	_____
____	Sure-Hire Cover Letters	10.95	_____

Résumés

____	100 Winning Résumés for $100,000+ Jobs	24.95	_____
____	175 High-Impact Résumés	10.95	_____
____	1500+ KeyWords for $100,000+ Jobs	14.95	_____
____	Asher's Bible of Executive Résumés	29.95	_____
____	Dynamite Résumés	14.95	_____
____	Electronic Résumé Revolution	12.95	_____
____	Electronic Résumés: Putting Your Résumé On-Line	19.95	_____
____	Electronic Résumés for the New Job Market	11.95	_____
____	Gallery of Best Résumés	16.95	_____
____	High Impact Résumés and Letters	19.95	_____
____	Résumé Catalog	15.95	_____
____	Résumé Shortcuts	14.95	_____
____	Résumés for Dummies	12.99	_____
____	Résumés That Knock 'Em Dead	10.95	_____
____	Sure-Hire Résumés	14.95	_____

Skills, Testing, Self-Assessment, Empowerment

____	7 Habits of Highly Effective People	14.00	_____
____	Discover the Best Jobs for You	12.95	_____
____	Do What You Are	16.95	_____
____	Do What You Love, the Money Will Follow	10.95	_____

Dress and Etiquette

____	110 Mistakes Working Women Make...	9.95	_____
____	Executive Etiquette in the New Workplace	14.95	_____
____	*New* Women's Dress For Success	12.99	_____
____	Red Socks Don't Work!	14.95	_____
____	Winning Image	17.95	_____

Networking and Power Building

____ Dynamite Networking For Dynamite Jobs	15.95	_____
____ Dynamite Tele-Search	12.95	_____
____ How to Work a Room	11.99	_____
____ Power to Get In	24.95	_____

Interviewing

____ 101 Dynamite Questions to Ask at Your Job Interview	14.95	_____
____ 101 Dynamite Answers to Interview Questions	12.95	_____
____ 111 Dynamite Ways to Ace Your Job Interview	13.95	_____
____ Dynamite Salary Negotiations	15.95	_____
____ Interview For Success	15.95	_____
____ Job Interviews For Dummies	12.99	_____

SUBTOTAL   _____

Virginia residents add 4½% sales tax   _____

POSTAGE/HANDLING ($5.00 for first
title plus 8% of SUBTOTAL over $30) $5.00

8% of SUBTOTAL over $30---------------------- _____

TOTAL ENCLOSED --------------------- _____

NAME _____

ADDRESS _____

_____

❑ I enclose check/moneyorder for $ _____ made payable to
IMPACT PUBLICATIONS.

❑ Please charge $ _____ to my credit card:

    ❑ Visa   ❑ MasterCard   ❑ American Express

    Card # _____

    Expiration date: _____/_____

    Signature _____

The On-Line Superstore & Warehouse
Hundreds of Terrific Career Resources Conveniently Available On the World Wide Web 24-Hours a Day, 365 Days a Year!

Ever wanted to know what are the newest and best books, directories, newsletters, wall charts, training programs, videos, CD-ROMs, computer software, and kits available to help you land a job, negotiate a higher salary, or start your own business? What about finding a job in Asia or relocating to San Francisco? Are you curious about how to find a job 24-hours a day by using the Internet or what you'll be doing five years from now? Trying to keep up-to-date on the latest career resources but not able to find the latest catalogs, brochures, or newsletters on today's "best of the best" resources?

Welcome to the first virtual career bookstore on the Internet. Now you're only a "click" away with Impact Publication's electronic solution to the resource challenge. Impact Publications, one of the nation's leading publishers and distributors of career resources, has launched its comprehensive "Career Superstore and Warehouse" on the Internet. The bookstore is jam-packed with the latest job and career resources on:

- Alternative jobs and careers
- Self-assessment
- Career planning and job search
- Employers
- Relocation and cities
- Resumes
- Cover Letters
- Dress, image, and etiquette
- Education
- Telephone
- Military
- Salaries
- Interviewing
- Nonprofits
- Empowerment
- Self-esteem
- Goal setting
- Executive recruiters
- Entrepreneurship
- Government
- Networking
- Electronic job search
- International jobs
- Travel
- Law
- Training and presentations
- Minorities
- Physically challenged

The bookstore also includes a new "Military Career Transition Center" and "School-to-Work Center."

"This is more than just a bookstore offering lots of product," say Drs. Ron and Caryl Krannich, two of the nation's leading career experts and authors and developers of this on-line bookstore. *"We're an important resource center for libraries, corporations, government, educators, trainers, and career counselors who are constantly defining and redefining this dynamic field. Of the thousands of career resources we review each year, we only select the 'best of the best.'"*

Visit this rich site and you'll quickly discover just about everything you ever wanted to know about finding jobs, changing careers, and starting your own business—including many useful resources that are difficult to find in local bookstores and libraries. The site also includes what's new and hot, tips for job search success, and monthly specials. Impact's Web address is:

http://www.impactpublications.com